FEARLESS
ENTERTAINING

■ **Laurence Sombke** ■

FEARLESS
ENTERTAINING

E. P. DUTTON  NEW YORK

Published in the United States by E. P. Dutton,
a division of Penguin Books USA Inc.,
2 Park Avenue, New York, N.Y. 10016.

Published simultaneously in Canada by
Fitzhenry and Whiteside, Limited, Toronto.

Library of Congress Cataloging-in-Publication Data

Sombke, Laurence.
Fearless entertaining.

1. Cookery, International.   2. Entertaining.
3. Menus.   I. Title.
TX725.A15572   1989   641.59   89-11858
ISBN: 0-525-48488-4

DESIGNED BY EARL TIDWELL

1   3   5   7   9   10   8   6   4   2

First Edition

■ Contents ■

CONTENTS

viii

■ Introduction ■

Fearless Entertaining is a cookbook and entertaining guide for people who think cooking and entertaining with friends at home is as much or more fun than going to an overpriced restaurant, a noisy bar, or a smoky nightclub.

I have created twenty-five theme-oriented dinner parties much the same as ones I have given in my own home. (Actually, they're not all dinners, but they are all meals.) Some are modeled after the theme restaurants like Sugar Reef in New York or Ed Debevik's in Chicago; others come from favorite ethnic, American regional, and international cuisines. I also drew inspiration from parties I worked when I was a caterer in New York.

Some of the menus are designed for special events. Let's say New Year's Eve is approaching and you're thinking about last year's dreadful party at the home of someone you barely knew and how much more fun an elegant dinner with friends would be. Turn to the Sparkling New Year's Eve chapter.

You serve a first course of smoked salmon that you buy and lay out on a pretty tray. Five minutes' work. Then there's blini with caviar. Caviar you buy at the smoked salmon store. Blini are "silver-dollar pancakes" all dressed up. They take 15 minutes to make. Rack of lamb with celeriac purée, another 30 minutes. Chocolate mousse takes 10 minutes to make and 12 hours to chill.

Now you can serve a truly impressive meal that took you 60 minutes to prepare and would cost you a fortune to order in a restaurant. No tax. No tip. No taxi rides to hell. No baby-sitter. Just your lovely home and wonderful friends. That's fearless entertaining.

The book is easy to use. I give you a three- to four-course menu, with easy-to-follow recipes, plus a step-by-step work routine called "Pulling It All Together," wine, beer, or other beverage recommendations, musical selections and advice on creating an ambience. Everything you've ever wanted to know about producing a successful dinner party is here. Of course, there is plenty of room for your own creativity.

There are some basic principles at work in this book. I expect most of you entertain on the weekend. You're too busy with your life during the week. I have made the recipes and instructions simple but not simpleminded. You will get great-tasting food but you won't have to spend the entire week cooking it. Most of these menus can be accomplished in an hour or two.

I have tried to keep these parties compact and manageable. I tell you to buy a pie or cake, or simply serve fruit for dessert. I encourage you to cut corners and make substitutions on your own to make these menus work for you.

Most of you already know how to follow recipes and cook new dishes. Many of you might consider yourselves "gourmet" cooks. But even really good home cooks have told me over the years that they have a hard time preparing the food *and* serving it on time at the right time. Professional chefs know how to plan this. The "Pulling It All Together" sections do the planning for you. Be sure to read them before you dive into the recipes.

I am a working journalist and spend most of my day researching and writing stories. My wife has a full-time job, and we also have a toddler. We don't have all day to cook or prepare elaborate events. My life is a lot like yours, except I'm probably a more experienced cook.

Most of the menus in *Fearless Entertaining* will cook enough food for four people, a few are for six to eight. This book isn't for couples or for singles only. It's for people who entertain a lot and are just looking for some new ideas, and it's for those of you who have been invited to everybody else's parties and now the big finger of reciprocity is pointing at you. It's your turn to entertain. Buy this book. Use it and enjoy yourself. Be fearless.

FEARLESS
ENTERTAINING

Spring Country Weekend

Make this meal: "When that April with his showers soote
The droughte of March hath perced to the roote."

SERVES 4

☐ Asparagus with Hollandaise Sauce
☐ Poached Salmon with Herb Sauce
☐ Buttered New Potatoes
☐ Strawberry Pound Cake

ASPARAGUS WITH HOLLANDAISE SAUCE

1 pound fresh asparagus
4 egg yolks
1 stick (½ cup) unsalted
    butter
2 tablespoons freshly squeezed
    lemon juice
¼ teaspoon salt
⅛ teaspoon cayenne pepper

1. Wash the asparagus and trim off any woody stems. Plunge the asparagus into a large pot of boiling water. Return to the boil and let cook 5 minutes. Drain and place on a plate.

2. Make the hollandaise. Half fill the bottom part of a double boiler with boiling water and put the top half over it. Keep the heat on medium-high just so the water continues to boil gently.

3. Put the egg yolks in the top half of the double boiler and stir like crazy for 2 minutes. Do not let the eggs get too hot or they will curdle.

4. Add one-third of the butter and stir as it melts. Add half of the remaining butter and stir until it melts. Add the rest of the butter and stir till it melts and the sauce becomes thick. Add the lemon juice, salt, and cayenne. Stir to form a smooth creamy sauce. Pour over the asparagus and serve.

1

POACHED SALMON WITH HERB SAUCE

FOR THE SALMON:

1 cup dry white wine
1 small carrot, peeled and chopped
1 small onion, peeled and chopped
1 tablespoon minced fresh parsley

1 bay leaf
½ teaspoon black pepper
4 salmon steaks, about 1½ to 2
    pounds total

1. Place 1 quart water, wine, carrot, onion, parsley, bay leaf, and black pepper in a fish poacher or pot in which you are going to poach the salmon steaks. Bring to a boil, reduce heat to medium-high, and simmer for 10 minutes.

2. Gently place the salmon steaks in the poaching liquid, cover, and continue cooking at medium-high heat for 10 minutes. Do not boil.

3. Turn off the heat. Salmon can rest in this liquid up to 20 minutes until you are ready to serve.

FOR THE HERB SAUCE:

½ cup minced fresh Italian flat-
    leafed parsley
1 large or 2 small shallots, peeled
    and chopped
1 tablespoon fresh or 1 teaspoon
    dried tarragon, or 1 tablespoon
    fresh or 1 teaspoon dried dill

1 tablespoon fresh or 1 teaspoon
    dried chives
1 clove garlic, peeled and minced
½ cup olive oil
3 tablespoons white wine vinegar
1 tablespoon Dijon or country
    French mustard

1. Place all of the ingredients in a food processor and whir to form a smooth dressing. Place in a bowl and serve with salmon.

BUTTERED NEW POTATOES

12 small new potatoes, washed and peeled
1 tablespoon butter

Salt and freshly ground black pepper to taste

1. Place the potatoes in a medium-sized saucepan and cover them with cold water. Bring the water to the boil, cover, and simmer for 10 to 15 minutes, or until potatoes are tender but firm.
2. Drain the potatoes, toss with the butter, salt, and pepper, and serve.

STRAWBERRY POUND CAKE

1 loaf pound cake, or 1 package of shortcake biscuits
1 quart fresh-picked local-grown strawberries

1 tablespoon granulated sugar
1 cup whipping cream

1. Slice the pound cake or shortcake biscuits into thin slices and set them aside.
2. Wash the strawberries in a large bowl of water to remove any sand or grit. Trim off the stems and slice the berries thin. Sprinkle the sugar on the strawberries, stir, and let the berries sit for 20 minutes. The sugar creates a juice for the berries.
3. Whip the cream until stiff. Lay a slice of cake on a plate. Spoon on a layer of strawberries and a layer of whipped cream. Do this twice more to make a triple-decker strawberry pound cake or shortcake.

Chances are that you have rushed up to your country house at the last minute on a Friday afternoon and your weekend guests are arriving any minute. No problem. Just remember to buy all the ingredients before you head out, and cook them when you arrive.

First prepare the strawberries and whipped cream. Cover and place them in the refrigerator until the very last minute.

Next make the court bouillon. This is a lot easier if you have a long metal fish poacher. Just place the vegetables, liquids, and seasonings in the poacher and turn it on.

Now, wash and pare the potatoes and the asparagus. Put them in their respective cooking containers and cover the potatoes with cold water.

Make the herb sauce, cover, and let rest at room temperature.

Just after your guests arrive and you have their gear stowed away, you can make the hollandaise. Stop whatever else you are doing and pay attention to this. Cover it carefully and keep it warm on the back of the stove.

Once everybody is ready to eat, cook the asparagus, and put the salmon and potatoes on to cook. Serve the asparagus with hollandaise as the first course.

Return to the kitchen. Drain the potatoes. Remove the salmon from its court bouillon and put it on individual plates. Add a potato or two to each plate. Spoon a bit of herb sauce next to the salmon. Serve.

Return to the kitchen and slice the pound cake or shortcake. Assemble the dessert and serve.

BEVERAGES. I would serve a young grassy white wine with this meal. A German or New York State Riesling or an Alsatian Gewürztraminer would be good. So would French Chablis, Sancerre, Vouvray, or Muscadet.

AMBIENCE. This meal seems to require a Laura Ashley–type look, but don't redecorate your house just for dinner. Calico or any floral pattern cloth napkins are a simple and lovely touch.

You won't have time to be too elaborate but I do think candles are nice because everyone will be a little road-weary and ready for a delicious meal that says spring.

■ Caribbean West Indies ■

Warm breezes. Palm trees. Red Stripe beer. Mon!

SERVES 4 TO 6

☐ Trade Winds Coconut Shrimp
☐ Jamaican Jerk Chicken
☐ Cuban Black Beans
☐ Antilles Rice
☐ Island Pineapple Dessert

TRADE WINDS COCONUT SHRIMP

1 pound medium shrimp, in the
  shell
2 eggs
⅔ cup packaged grated coconut
1½ cups all-purpose flour

½ teaspoon salt
1 cup flat beer
1 quart vegetable oil for frying

1. Wash and peel the shrimp, leaving the tails on.

2. Beat the eggs in a medium-sized mixing bowl. Add the coconut and stir to blend well.

3. In a separate bowl, mix the flour and salt. Add this mixture and the beer to the eggs and whisk to form a smooth batter. Let rest for 20 minutes, whisking occasionally.

4. Heat the oil to 375°F. in a large heavy pot, wok, or electric skillet. 375°F. is the point at which the oil will just begin to smoke. If it smokes a lot, it is much too hot and the fish will burn. Drop a piece of batter into the oil. If it sputters and turns a nice golden brown, the oil is ready.

5. Dip the shrimp in the batter and fry in small batches in the oil. Drain the shrimp on paper towels and keep warm.

JAMAICAN JERK CHICKEN

8 to 12 chicken thighs
2 tablespoons ground allspice
3 to 4 hot green chili peppers,
	Scotch bonnies, jalapeño,
	serrano, or long green cayenne
	peppers, chopped
3 scallions, trimmed and chopped

¼ cup light soy sauce
1 tablespoon fresh ginger, peeled
¼ teaspoon each cinnamon and
	cloves
½ teaspoon each salt and black
	pepper

1. Place the thighs in a large glass or ceramic cake pan or casserole dish. Place the remaining ingredients and ½ cup water in a food processor and whir until a smooth sauce forms.

2. Pour the sauce over the chicken, coat the pieces thoroughly, and let marinate for at least 1 hour at room temperature or overnight in the refrigerator.

3. The most authentic and flavorful way to make Jamaican Jerk Chicken is to cook it over a slow smoky fire outdoors. Build a charcoal or wood fire in a hooded barbecue grill. When the coals are gray, move them all over to one side of the grill. Place the chicken pieces on the side of the grill opposite the coals and at the highest point away from the fire. Cover the grill, close all the vents and let the meat roast for 30 to 40 minutes.

4. If you are using your inside oven, preheat it to 325°F. Drain the marinade from the chicken and place the thighs in a roasting pan. Cover with foil and roast for 1 hour.

CUBAN BLACK BEANS

2 tablespoons vegetable oil
1 medium onion, peeled and
    chopped fine
1 green or red bell pepper, cored,
    seeded, and chopped fine
1 stalk celery, chopped fine
3 cloves garlic, peeled and minced

1 bay leaf
3 ounces smoked ham or smoked
    pork chop, chopped
One 16-ounce can prepared black
    beans
1/2 teaspoon black pepper
1/4 teaspoon salt

1. In a medium-sized saucepan, heat the oil over medium heat for 1 minute. Add the onion, bell pepper, celery, and garlic and sauté for 3 to 5 minutes.

2. Add the bay leaf, smoked ham, beans, 1/2 cup water, salt, and pepper. Stir and reduce the heat to medium-low. Cook, covered, for 15 minutes, adding more water if the beans get too dry. Stir frequently.

ANTILLES RICE

1/2 cup each chopped fresh parsley,
    scallions with green tops,
    celery, and green bell pepper
2 cloves garlic, peeled and minced
2 tablespoons vegetable oil

5 strands Spanish saffron
1 cup short- or long-grain white
    rice
Salt and black pepper to taste
2 cups chicken stock or water

1. In a medium-sized saucepan with a tight-fitting lid, sauté the parsley, scallions, celery, bell pepper, and garlic in the oil over medium heat 3 to 5 minutes.

2. Add the saffron, rice, salt, pepper, and chicken stock or water. Cover and bring to the boil for 1 minute. Turn the heat to very low and let the rice cook for 10 to 15 minutes, or until the liquid has been absorbed by the rice. Do not stir.

3. Turn off the heat and let the rice sit, covered, for 10 minutes. Stir briefly before serving to fluff up the rice.

ISLAND PINEAPPLE DESSERT

1 whole fresh ripe pineapple
2 star fruits (optional)
2 tablespoons grated coconut
    (optional)

2 tablespoons dark rum (optional)

1. A perfectly ripe fresh pineapple and a good sharp knife are all you need to make this dessert a success. I have listed the star fruits, coconut, and dark rum as optional additions; they are not totally necessary.

2. Lay the pineapple down on your cutting board and cut it in half lengthwise. Cut each half again in half lengthwise. Leave the spiky stems on each quarter.

3. Lay 1 pineapple quarter on the cutting board with the inside facing up. With your knife, cut the woody central core lengthwise away from the tender fruit. Place your free hand on top of the fruit and cut the fruit away from the outer skin.

4. Remove the fruit, still in one long piece, from the skin. Cut in $1/2$-inch crosswise slices. Return the slices to the skin, which has now become the plate, so to speak, for the slices. Repeat with other quarters.

5. If you want to add the other items, slice the star fruits thin and place a slice or two on top of each pineapple quarter. Sprinkle with coconut and rum and serve.

Make the marinade and pour over the chicken pieces. If you are going to cook the meat on the barbecue grill, start the fire, and when it is ready put the meat on to cook.

Peel the shrimp and make the batter. Then cook the black beans and dirty rice. Both can be made up to an hour ahead of time and kept warm. You should also prepare the pineapple dessert before your guests arrive.

When your guest do come, greet them and check on your chicken. It should be done by now. Remove from the oven or grill and keep warm.

Get everyone to the table and then fry and serve the shrimp. Go back to the kitchen and make sure the chicken, rice, and beans are warm.

Spread the rice out on a large platter. Place the chicken on top. Put the beans in a warm bowl, and bring everything to the table.

Clear the table and serve the dessert. For coffee, to be authentic, get freshly ground Jamaican Blue Mountain coffee. It is especially aromatic and flavorful.

BEVERAGES. The three main beer brands from the Caribbean are Red Stripe from Jamaica, Banks from Barbados, and Carib from Trinidad and Tobago. All are light refreshing beers with a little more flavor than Budweiser or Miller's.

Colorful Caribbean cocktails have become very popular with the spread of Caribbean restaurants. Here are three good standby cocktails that are easy to make.

Cuba Libre: Fill a highball glass with ice, add 1 ounce light rum, squeeze a wedge of lemon or lime into the glass, fill with Coke.

Daiquiri: In a blender, for each drink, place 2 ice cubes, 1 ounce light rum, 2 ounces sweet-and-sour mix. Blend until smooth and pour into stemmed glasses.

Piña Colada: In a blender or mixing cup, for each drink, place 2 ice cubes, 1 ounce light rum, 1 ounce cream of coconut, 2 ounces pineapple juice. Blend or shake mixing cup 10 times, pour into tall thin glasses.

Along with the cocktails, set out bowls of plantain chips, which are just like potato chips except they are made with plantains, a type of savory banana.

AMBIENCE. Here's where the fun starts. Ask your guests to bring slides of their last trip to the Islands, or borrow slides from the library of a West Indian tourist agency. Make a vegetable sculpture with shaggy brown coconuts and tall green sugar cane. Try to make the room look like a beachside cabana with palm leaves laced with twinkling lights and backyard Japanese lanterns.

You might start the evening with some sedate calypso or steel drum band music. As the evening progresses, switch to reggae music featuring Bob Marley, Jimmy Cliff, or Peter Tosh.

■ Heartland ■

A MIDWESTERN MEAL

*For all you closet pork chop lovers. And you thought
the Midwest was just white bread and Jell-O salads.*

SERVES 4

- ☐ Cold Cherry Soup
- ☐ Pan-Grilled Iowa Pork Chops
- ☐ Warm German Potato Salad
- ☐ Buttered Green String Beans
- ☐ Pineapple Upside-Down Cake

COLD CHERRY SOUP

1½ pounds fresh or frozen dark
    sweet cherries, pitted
Juice of 1 lemon
¼ teaspoon each ground
    cinnamon, nutmeg, coriander

¼ cup granulated sugar
¼ cup kirschwasser (optional)
2 cups sour cream or a mixture of
    sour cream and plain yogurt

    1. Place the cherries and their juice in a 2- to 3-quart saucepan. If you are
using fresh cherries, you may need to add up to ½ cup water. Add the lemon
juice, spices, and sugar. Cook over medium heat for 5 minutes, stirring often.
Turn off the heat and let the cherries cool to lukewarm.
    2. Place the cherry mixture in a food processor and whir until smooth.
Add the kirschwasser and sour cream. Stir until smooth. Put the soup in the
refrigerator and chill for 1 hour.

PAN-GRILLED IOWA PORK CHOPS

4 center cut pork loin chops, 1½
    inches thick
2 tablespoons olive or corn oil
½ teaspoon dried thyme or
    rosemary

¼ teaspoon each salt and freshly
    ground black pepper

1. Place the chops on a platter. Mix the oil, herbs, salt, and pepper in a small bowl. Rub this mixture on the chops and let them rest, covered, at room temperature for 15 minutes.

2. Place a 9-inch heavy-duty cast-iron skillet over medium-high heat for 5 minutes. Put the pork chops in the skillet; no extra oil is necessary. Pan-grill the chops for 3 minutes, turn, and grill another 3 minutes. These chops will be medium, just past pink. (Pork does not need to be overcooked the way it was years ago.) Remove from the pan, cover with foil, and keep warm.

WARM GERMAN POTATO SALAD

6 medium-sized all-purpose white
    or red potatoes
4 strips thick-cut bacon
1 medium onion, peeled and
    chopped fine
2 stalks celery, chopped fine
¼ cup minced fresh parsley

¼ cup vinegar
1 teaspoon dry mustard or
    1 tablespoon prepared mustard
¼ teaspoon each salt and freshly
    ground black pepper

1. Wash and peel the potatoes. Place in a saucepan, cover with water, and boil for 15 minutes. Drain and cool.

2. Fry the bacon in a large skillet until crispy. Remove from pan, leaving ¼ cup of the bacon drippings in the pan.

3. Return the pan to the stove and place over medium heat. Add the onion, celery, and parsley to the pan and sauté for 5 minutes, until soft. Add

the vinegar, mustard, salt, and pepper. Crumble the bacon and add that. Cook this mixture, stirring often, to form a creamy sauce.

4. Slice the potatoes into bite-sized pieces and add to the sauce. Stir.

BUTTERED GREEN STRING BEANS

1 pound fresh green string beans
1 tablespoon unsalted butter

1. Look for fresh green beans that are bright green, unblemished, and slender. Wash them and trim off the tips and stems.

2. Bring a quart of water to the boil in a large pot. Add the beans and return to the boil for 5 minutes. Drain and plunge the beans into cold water. Drain.

3. Put the pot back on the stove over medium heat. Add the butter and the beans. Toss until beans are hot and coated with butter. Serve.

PINEAPPLE UPSIDE-DOWN CAKE

1 cup brown sugar
3 tablespoons unsalted butter
One 1-pound can pineapple chunks, drained (save the juice)
1 cup granulated sugar
3 eggs, separated

1/2 cup pineapple juice from the chunks
1 1/2 cups all-purpose flour
2 teaspoons baking powder
1/4 teaspoon salt
1 teaspoon vanilla extract

1. Preheat the oven to 350°F. Mix the crumbled brown sugar and butter on the bottom of a 9-inch black cast-iron skillet. Lay the pineapple chunks over that.

2. Add the granulated sugar to the egg yolks and beat with a whisk for 2 minutes. Add the pineapple juice, flour, baking powder, salt, and vanilla. Beat thoroughly.

3. Whip the egg whites until they are stiff. Fold them into the batter, and pour over the pineapple/sugar mixture in the skillet.

4. Place the skillet in the oven and bake for 30 minutes, or until a toothpick comes out clean when inserted in the center of the cake. Remove from the oven and let cool 30 minutes.

5. Run a knife around the edges of the cake to loosen it from the skillet. Place a large serving plate facedown over the cake in the skillet. Holding them together tightly, invert the skillet over the plate. The cake should plop down out of the skillet onto the serving platter.

Make the cake earlier in the day or the day before. It improves with age and you need to use the skillet for the pork chops.

Next make the cold cherry soup because it has to chill in the refrigerator. This could also be made the day before.

Marinate the pork chops in the oil and spices. Wash and trim the green beans.

Boil the potatoes for the German potato salad and start to fry the bacon. When the potatoes are cool enough to handle, finish the potato salad and keep warm. Cook the green beans and plunge them into cold water.

The final assembly: Grill the pork chops and keep them warm. Serve the cold soup. Go back to the kitchen and toss the green beans in the hot butter. Bring everything to the table.

BEVERAGES. The best wines to serve with a heartland meal are the German-style white wines. They are crisp and dry but still with a little taste of fruit. Try Johannisberg Riesling, Gewürztraminer, or the fruitier Seyval Blanc. Several midwestern states, Michigan and Missouri in particular, have good native wines.

There are several small breweries still in operation in the Midwest that make very good beer. Pickett in Dubuque, Iowa, Point in Stevens Point, Wisconsin, Leinenkugel's of Chippewa Falls, Wisconsin, and Little King's in Cincinnati, are just a few. Or serve St. Pauli Girl, Beck's, or Heineken.

AMBIENCE. There is no typical midwestern scene because the area is so large and varied that it is impossible to generalize. You would want to set the table with things that are understated, sturdy, and timeless. Clean Scandinavian designs or blue willow patterns are good for the plates. Get tall pilsener glasses for the beer and Victorian-style cut-glass goblets for wine.

Prairie wildflowers like black-eyed Susans or daisies would make a nice floral arrangement.

Ragtime music is midwestern because Scott Joplin was born in Sedalia, Missouri, and played piano in St. Louis. Kansas City was a major spot for jazz in the forties thanks to the big bands. After the meal, sit back and listen to a cassette tape of Garrison Keillor's *A Prairie Home Companion*.

■ Spanish Tapas Party ■

*Tapas—the varied Spanish bar snacks, all designed to be finger food—
are perfect cocktail party fare. But don't expect to be hungry for dinner
afterward!*

SERVES 6 TO 8

- ☐ Tortilla Española—Spanish potato omelet
- ☐ Pisto Manchego—Ratatouille Spanish style
- ☐ Grilled Chorizo—Smoked pork sausage with Spanish paprika
- ☐ Gambas à la Plancha—Grilled shrimp
- ☐ Pan con Tomate—Tomato canapé like bruschetta

TORTILLA ESPAÑOLA

1 medium onion, peeled and
    chopped fine
½ cup plus 2 tablespoons olive oil
4 large potatoes, peeled and cut
    into thin slices

6 eggs
Salt and pepper to taste

1. In a heavy 9-inch skillet, sauté the onion in ½ cup olive oil over medium heat for 5 minutes. Add the potato slices, cover the skillet, and continue cooking for 20 minutes. Keep the heat low to avoid browning the potatoes.

2. Combine the eggs, salt, and pepper in a bowl. Beat the eggs until they are foamy. Remove the potatoes and onion from the pan and mix them into the eggs.

3. Scrape the skillet clean with a spatula and return it to medium heat. Add the remaining 2 tablespoons olive oil. Pour the potato-and-egg mixture into the pan, spreading it around to form a nice flat cake.

4. When the eggs begin to set and the potatoes begin to brown on the bottom, place a plate facedown over the rim of the skillet. Invert the skillet

and the plate, allowing the potato omelet to drop onto the plate. Slide the omelet back into the pan, browned side up, and brown the other side. Cook another 5 to 10 minutes over low heat.

5. Remove the tortilla from the skillet, cover, and let rest. Slice into small wedges and serve at room temperature.

PISTO MANCHEGO

3 tablespoons olive oil
1 large green pepper, cored, seeded, and coarsely chopped
1 large onion, peeled and chopped
1 medium zucchini, trimmed and chopped
1 small eggplant, trimmed and cubed

5 cloves garlic, peeled and minced
3 medium fresh tomatoes, peeled and chopped
1 tablespoon minced fresh parsley
Salt and pepper to taste

1. Warm the olive oil in a heavy skillet. Add the green pepper, onion, zucchini, and eggplant. Sauté for 5 minutes over medium heat.

2. Add the garlic and cook another 5 minutes. Add the tomatoes, parsley, salt, and pepper. Cook over medium heat for 25 minutes. Cover and let cool to room temperature.

GRILLED CHORIZO

1 pound chorizo sausage (available in Mexican and Latin American markets, and some gourmet shops)

1. Preheat the broiler. Place the chorizo on a broiling pan and cook them 4 to 6 inches away from the heat source for 10 minutes. Turn them occasionally to be sure they brown all over.

2. Allow the sausages to cool 5 minutes and cut into thin slices.

GAMBAS À LA PLANCHA

1½ to 2 pounds fresh medium to
   large shrimp, shells on
1 cup olive oil

4 cloves garlic, peeled and minced
1 cup minced fresh parsley

1. Wash the shrimp, drain them, and allow them to dry.

2. Find the largest and heaviest skillet you have. A well-seasoned wok or a heavy cast-iron skillet are the best. Heat the skillet over medium-high heat for 3 minutes. Add ¼ cup of the olive oil and heat it for 15 seconds. Add a quarter of the shrimp and sauté over medium-high heat for 3 to 5 minutes. Add a quarter of the minced garlic and ¼ cup of the parsley. Sauté another 1 to 2 minutes, stirring frequently.

3. Continue cooking the shrimp in batches, using a quarter of each ingredient in each batch. Keep finished shrimp warm. Serve immediately.

PAN CON TOMATE

1 large loaf crusty French or Italian
   bread
2 medium tomatoes, peeled and
   cored

½ cup fruity olive oil
4 cloves garlic, peeled and minced

1. Slice the bread into ½-inch-thick pieces. Lightly toast the slices. Lay the slices on a large cookie sheet. Preheat the broiler.

2. Chop the tomatoes. Drain out as much of the juice as possible. Blend the tomatoes, olive oil, and garlic and mash the mixture in a heavy bowl with the back of a wooden spoon.

3. Spread each bread slice with a dab of the mixture. Place the slices under the broiler and broil for 30 seconds. Serve.

Make the tortilla and the pisto early, long before your guests arrive. They can both benefit from being made several hours ahead of time to give the flavors a chance to mingle.

Place the chorizo on the broiler pan, prepare the topping for the pan con tomate, and chop the garlic and parsley for the shrimp.

When the guests arrive, set out bowls of toasted whole almonds, a plate of Manchego cheese, and slices of crusty bread.

Once everyone is comfortable, grill the chorizo, sauté the shrimp, and broil the pan con tomate. Place them all on separate platters and bring all the food, including the tortilla and the pisto, to the table.

Tapas are served in Spain the way bar snacks are served in the United States. You snack on tapas while you drink. For your party, spread the tapas out buffet style. If you have a bar, spread them out on that. Brown ceramic bowls called cazuelas are the best serving dishes to use. Offer little forks and plenty of napkins, especially for the shrimp, which are best enjoyed as finger food. Put out bowls for the shrimp shells.

BEVERAGES. The best drink to serve with tapas is well-chilled dry Spanish sherry, either fino or Manzanilla. La Ina, Tio Pepe, and Infantes de Orleans Borbon are three popular brands. It must be refrigerator-cold to be good. Serve it in tiny little wineglasses.

After sherry, the other choice would be cold beer. San Miguel is Spanish beer, but it is made in the Philippines for the American market.

Spanish white wines are similar to Italian white wines, light and pleasant. But Spanish red wines, particularly those from Rioja or Penedès are full-bodied and a very good buy.

AMBIENCE. Spanish tapas bars are colorful and crowded. A good bar in Spain is judged by the amount of litter on the floor. You wouldn't want to go into a place where no one else cares to go. I don't suggest littering your rooms, but I do suggest a casual atmosphere. Bullfight posters are actually very popular on the walls of bars in Spain, so you might try one.

Some guitar music performed by Andrés Segovia would be a good way to start the party while everyone is in a mellow mood. But once things get going, put on the flamenco, which is true barroom music, most authentically performed by gypsies and singers from Sevilla or from Aigues-Mortes, France.

■ Lawn Concert Picnic ■

*This kind of picnic should be elegant enough to make the evening special,
but simple enough so that you don't have to bring
your whole kitchen with you.
This menu fits the bill nicely.*

SERVES 4

- ☐ Crudités with Tapenade
- ☐ Tabouleh Salad
- ☐ Herb-Roasted Cornish Hens
- ☐ Fresh Berries and Whipped Cream

CRUDITÉS WITH TAPENADE

3 carrots
1 medium cucumber
1 each red and green bell pepper

1 bunch radishes
3 stalks celery
1 bulb fennel (if available)

1. Peel the carrots and cucumber and slice them into sticks. Core and seed the peppers and slice them into strips. Wash the radishes and pare off any stems. Slice the celery and fennel into strips. Place the vegetables in plastic bags and refrigerate them.

FOR THE TAPENADE:
One 2-ounce tin anchovies, rinsed
    and soaked in milk to remove
    some of the saltiness
½ cup pitted oil-cured black olives

2 tablespoons capers
¼ cup olive oil
Juice of ½ lemon

1. Place the anchovies, olives, and capers in a food processor and whir to make a creamy paste.
2. With the motor running on low, add the olive oil, drop by drop, until

21

the mixture thickens like mayonnaise. Add the lemon juice and whir for 1 second.

3. Remove the tapenade to a container and cover. At serving time, everyone dips the raw vegetables in the tapenade.

TABOULEH SALAD

1 cup bulgur
½ cup minced fresh parsley
½ cup minced scallions
1 tablespoon minced fresh mint or
    1 teaspoon dried mint
2 ripe tomatoes, cored and chopped
    fine

Juice of 1 lemon
⅓ cup olive oil
Salt and freshly ground black
    pepper to taste

1. Place the bulgur in a medium-sized salad bowl. Add 2 cups hot tap water and let rest for 30 minutes. The grain will soak up the water and expand.

2. Add the rest of the ingredients and stir to blend well. Cover and refrigerate.

HERB-ROASTED CORNISH HENS

2 Cornish hens, cut into quarters
3 tablespoons olive oil
2 teaspoons each dried oregano and
    thyme

½ teaspoon each salt and pepper

1. Rub the Cornish hens all over with olive oil. Sprinkle them with the oregano, thyme, salt, and pepper.

2. Place the hen quarters on a broiler pan and broil 4 to 6 inches from the heat source for 15 to 20 minutes. Remove and let cool.

FRESH BERRIES AND WHIPPED CREAM

1 pint fresh, in season raspberries,
  blackberries, strawberries, or
  blueberries, or a combination

1 cup whipping cream
1 teaspoon granulated sugar
  (optional)

1. Wash the berries in a bowl of water and pick over to remove any blemished ones or any stems and twigs. Drain. Place in a plastic container.

2. Whip the cream until stiff, beating in the sugar at the end. Place in a separate plastic container, cover, and refrigerate.

This is another one of those do-everything-ahead meals. It is also a meal that you can make after work in less than an hour, giving you plenty of time to get to the concert site.

Prepare the Cornish hens and put them in the oven first thing. While the hens are cooking, pour the hot water over the bulgur and give it time to fluff up. Chop the vegetables for the tabouleh and put them in a large salad bowl.

Prepare the vegetables for the crudités, and make the tapenade.

Wash the berries and whip the cream. Put them in separate containers and chill them.

Blend the bulgur with the flavorings, oil, and vegetables for the tabouleh. Mix well and place in a sealed plastic container.

By now the hens are ready to remove from the oven. Let them cool and double-wrap them in aluminum foil.

Pack everything in a picnic basket and take it to the concert site. If everything is chilled and well wrapped, and you are heading straight to the concert, you won't need a cooler. This food will be safe to eat at room temperature. The only thing you might want to keep in a small cooler is the whipped cream.

BEVERAGES. Wine is a classic and wonderful thing to bring to a lawn concert picnic but too much wine may make you too sleepy to be awake for the last movement. If you do bring wine, choose a very cold bottle of very good white wine. I would prefer an icy bottle of French or California Chardonnay.

Probably the very best beverage is bottled water, both bubbly and still. I would get unflavored water so that it does not clash with any of the flavors of the food.

AMBIENCE. Whether it is at Tanglewood, Ravinia, or the Great Lawn of Central Park, the most important thing to remember about a lawn concert picnic is that you are going to have to carry to the concert site anything you are going to eat. You will want to be very economical with what you bring.

Naturally you will want to carry your picnic in a classic old-fashioned wicker picnic basket. All of the utensils are already in there. Be sure to add a colorful cloth to spread the picnic on, colorful cloth napkins, and a blanket to sit on.

Try to dress up the event by bringing charming salt and pepper shakers or napkin rings.

Eat as soon as you get to the concert site. There is nothing worse than people munching away during the first movement. The music from the stage should be ample.

■ Eastern Mediterranean ■

*The foods of the Aegean, the Levant, and the
Nile are meant to be shared with friends.*

SERVES 4

☐ Mezes—Assorted appetizers of hummus, baba
  ghanoush, stuffed grape leaves, peppers, olives, feta
  cheese, cucumbers, tomatoes, and pita bread.
☐ Lamb Shish Kabobs
☐ Rice Pilaf
☐ Melon

MEZES

2 cucumbers, peeled and cut into
  strips lengthwise
2 ripe tomatoes, cored and sliced
One 8-ounce can stuffed grape
  leaves
$1/2$ cup peperoncini peppers

$1/2$ cup black Calamata olives
$1/4$ pound feta cheese
8 pita breads, warmed and
  quartered
1 recipe each hummus and baba
  ghanoush

HUMMUS

One 16-ounce can garbanzo beans,
  drained
8 ounces tahini (sesame paste)

$1/4$ cup fruity olive oil
1 clove garlic, peeled and minced
Juice of 1 lemon

1. Place the garbanzo beans and $1/2$ cup water in a food processor and
grind to a smooth paste. Add the tahini, olive oil, garlic, and lemon juice.
Grind for a few seconds until all ingredients are blended and you get a smooth
paste.

26 2. Place the hummus in a bowl, cover, and refrigerate.

BABA GHANOUSH

1 large fresh eggplant
4 ounces tahini (sesame paste)
3 tablespoons olive oil

1 clove garlic, peeled and minced
Juice of 1 lemon

1. Trim the stem and end off the eggplant. Cut it in half lengthwise and place on an oiled cookie sheet. Bake in a 375°F. oven for 1 hour. Cool.

2. Scoop the eggplant meat away from the skin and place in a food processor. Add the tahini, olive oil, garlic, and lemon juice. Process a few seconds until you get a smooth creamy paste. Remove from the processor, cover, and chill.

LAMB SHISH KABOBS

1½ to 2 pounds shoulder lamb
   chops
½ cup red wine
Juice of 1 lemon
⅓ cup olive oil

½ teaspoon each salt and pepper
1 teaspoon dried oregano
1 clove garlic, peeled and minced
⅛ teaspoon ground cinnamon

1. Trim the fat and bone away from the lamb chops. Cut into 1-inch cubes. Place in a large bowl.

2. Add the remaining ingredients to the bowl of lamb cubes. Stir and coat the meat with the marinade. Cover and let rest 1 hour at room temperature or in the refrigerator overnight.

3. Divide the meat into eight portions and thread each portion onto a small skewer. Broil the meat in the oven broiler or on a hibachi for 7 to 8 minutes, turning often and basting with the remaining marinade.

RICE PILAF

2 tablespoons each butter and
    olive oil
¼ cup orzo or other tiny pasta
¾ cup long-grain white rice
2 tablespoons golden raisins

2 tablespoons pignoli nuts,
    sunflower seeds, or almond
    slices
2 cups chicken or beef stock

1. Melt the butter and warm the olive oil over medium heat in a 2-quart saucepan. Add the orzo and rice and sauté for 3 minutes, stirring often, until the grains are browned.

2. Add the raisins, nuts, and stock. Bring the mixture to the boil. Cover, reduce heat to very low, and cook for 15 minutes. Turn off the heat and let rest for 10 minutes.

MELON

1. Try to serve a melon that is out of the ordinary. Look for Persian, Canary, Charentais, Ogen, or baby yellow watermelon.

2. To serve, cut the melon into very thin strips and remove the rind. Cut the watermelon into thin sheets and remove the seeds and rind.

Make the baba ghanoush and hummus first. While the eggplant is in the oven baking, you can make the hummus and put the lamb cubes in to marinate. All this can be done the day before.

Prepare the melon, sprinkle it with a tablespoon of lemon juice to keep it fresh, cover it, and place it in the refrigerator. I personally prefer melon that is "shade" temperature, that is, as if it has been sitting in the shade of a tree rather than the icy cold of a refrigerator. Refrigerator cold dulls some of the melon's earthy succulence.

Put the pilaf on to cook. Prepare the vegetables and lay out the mezes on a large platter. Cook the lamb shish kabobs, cover, and keep warm.

BEVERAGES. When your guests arrive, you might want to hand them a glass of ouzo, the licorice-tasting liquor from Greece. A jigger or shot of ouzo on ice topped with water in a tall glass is a good way to enjoy this distinctive drink.

The wines of Greece are good choices for this meal. Retsina, the resiny-tasting white wine, served ice cold, is perfect but not for everyone's taste. Red wines from Greece tend to be a little better than the whites and they can use a slight chilling.

Turkish coffee that is boiled three times in a long-handled metal cup is the ideal way to end this meal. Any fully stocked gourmet shop will have all the equipment and the coffee that you need.

AMBIENCE. There are many cultures, nationalities, languages, and religions in the eastern Mediterranean but they all share a common table. Tangy feta cheese and the flat pita bread are some of the oldest foods known by mankind and they have been eaten in this region during biblical times and before. Greeks, Jews, Turks, and Arabs all eat some of these foods.

So you can choose your ethnic party theme. Maybe a *Zorba the Greek* motif with taverna music and dancing. Or a *Lawrence of Arabia* tents-on-the-desert theme, or an Egyptian boat on the Nile approach.

Whatever theme you choose, serve all the food except the melon at the same time. Place the platter of mezes in the center of the table. Spread the rice pilaf on another platter and lay the shish kabobs on the pilaf. Have a third plate for the pita bread. Give everybody a plate and let them dig in.

■ New Wave Pizza Party ■

These pizzas fall into the category of contemporary updates
of old favorites.

SERVES 4

Individual 8-inch pizzas that your guests create themselves. You make the dough and provide a large selection of toppings. Your guests assemble their favorite pizza combinations, mix and match, share at the table, and invent new pizza taste sensations.

☐ New Wave Pizzas
☐ Radicchio, Arugula, and Endive Salad
☐ Ice Cream

NEW WAVE PIZZAS

Pizza dough can easily be made at home. But if you are really pressed for time, frozen bread dough, available in your supermarket frozen food case, is an acceptable substitute.

PIZZA DOUGH FOR SIX 8-INCH PIZZAS:

2 tablespoons dry baking yeast
1 teaspoon sugar
1/4 cup fruity olive oil, plus
    additional for oiling bowl,
    pans

1 teaspoon salt
3 cups flour
1 cup cornmeal for dusting baking
    pans

1. Dissolve the yeast in 1 1/4 cups warm water and add the sugar. Stir this mixture well and let rest 5 minutes. Add the oil, salt, and flour and stir to form a ball.
2. Place the ball on a well-floured flat work surface and knead the dough

31

for 10 minutes. Clean the mixing bowl and spread it with 1 tablespoon olive oil.

3. Place the dough ball in the bowl, turning to coat with oil. Cover and let dough rise in a warm place for 1 hour. Punch down, re-form into a ball, and let rise another 30 minutes.

4. Divide the dough into 6 equal portions. Roll out the dough balls into 8-inch circles with a well-floured rolling pin and place them into individual cake or pie tins that have been rubbed with olive oil and sprinkled with cornmeal.

5. Preheat the oven to 500°F. Top the pizzas with a variety of your favorite items and bake on the bottom of a gas oven or on the lowest shelf of an electric oven for 10 minutes. Remove and serve.

TOPPINGS:

Herbs—one small bunch each fresh basil, fresh rosemary, dried oregano, stems removed and chopped

Cheese—4 ounces freshly grated Parmesan and/or Romano; 8 ounces fresh mozzarella, shredded; 4 ounces crumbled chèvre; 4 ounces sliced smoked provolone

Vegetables—8 ounces pizza sauce (commercial or homemade); 1 cup diced red, yellow, or green bell peppers; 8 ounces sautéed button mushrooms, or 1 ounce dried porcini

mushrooms soaked for 20 minutes in hot water; 2 small Italian or Japanese eggplants sliced 1/4 inch thick and sautéed in olive oil; 1/2 cup finely chopped onion; 5 cloves peeled garlic, minced or thinly sliced; 3 medium-sized fresh tomatoes, sliced thin

Meat—cooked and crumbled sweet Italian sausage with fennel; pepperoni; fried bacon, drained and crumbled

Olive oil—small bottles of extra virgin and virgin oil

QUICK PIZZA SAUCE

1 medium onion, peeled and
    chopped fine
3 tablespoons fruity olive oil
1 clove garlic, peeled and minced
One 16-ounce can tomato sauce

1 teaspoon each dried basil and
    oregano
½ teaspoon each salt and ground
    black pepper

1. Sauté the onion in the olive oil over medium-high heat for 5 minutes. Add the garlic and sauté another 3 minutes. Add the tomato sauce, herbs, salt, and pepper. Bring to a boil. Reduce heat and simmer 10 minutes.

RADICCHIO, ARUGULA, AND ENDIVE SALAD

1 small head red radicchio
1 bunch arugula
2 heads Belgian endive
3 tablespoons extra virgin Italian
    olive oil

1 tablespoon red wine or balsamic
    vinegar
¼ teaspoon each salt and pepper

1. Wash the radicchio, arugula, and endives, separating the heads and removing any woody stems. Drain and dry with paper towels.

2. In a large wooden salad bowl, mix the olive oil with the vinegar, salt, and pepper, whisking to form a creamy dressing. Add the radicchio, arugula, and endive to the dressing and toss.

If you are going to make your own pizza dough, make that first because it takes two hours for the mixing and rising process. You can certainly make the dough the night before and refrigerate it until you are ready to use it. Simply remove it from the refrigerator 1 hour before you plan to form it into pizza shapes. If you are using frozen bread dough, follow package instructions and remove it from the freezer several hours before using to thaw and rise.

Next make the sauce and assemble and prepare all the topping ingredients. Put the toppings in individual bowls and cover with plastic wrap. Allow yourself an hour for this job. Make the salad dressing and prepare the greens, but toss at the table when ready to serve.

As your guests arrive, explain to them that they are going to make their own pizzas. Give each of them an apron and demonstrate how it is done. Encourage them to make combinations that go beyond their customary pizza parlor favorites. You should handle baking the pizzas in the oven, pulling them out, and slicing them. Serve the salad after everyone has tasted his or her own pizza and eyeballed the rest.

BEVERAGES. As your guests arrive, serve them a selection of Italian cocktails:

Campari and soda: Fill a tall thin highball glass with ice. Add 1½ ounces Campari and fill the glass with club soda or seltzer. Garnish with an orange slice.

Negroni: Fill a tall thin highball glass with ice. Add 1 ounce gin or vodka, 1 ounce Campari, 1 ounce sweet vermouth (preferably Punt e Mes) top with club soda or seltzer, and garnish with a lemon twist.

For wine, get beyond the usual inexpensive white wines and straw-wrapped Chianti and try something better. Italy has some other good wines that you should try, both red and white:

White: Corvo from Sicily, Verdicchio from the Adriatic Marches, Pinot Grigio from Friuli or Pinot Bianco from the Veneto, the region around Venice.

Red: Try the wines of Piemonte, such as Barbera d'Asti, Dolcetto, or

Gattinara. Instead of Chianti, try an Italian Cabernet from several regions in Italy.

AMBIENCE. A pizza party should be relaxed and fun. Think Italian wedding music like Mario Lanza, Tony Bennett, "Sorrento," and "The Isle of Capri." A red-checkered tablecloth will be obvious but colorful and appropriate.

Set out two different wineglasses for each guest so that they can try a red or a white wine with their pizza. Make a centerpiece of succulent vegetables like eggplant, garlic, onions, and peppers.

■ Dixie Truckstop ■

*Everyone loves this food, but your cooking is probably better
than most you find on the road.*

SERVES 4

☐ Cajun Fried Chicken with Pecan Gravy
☐ Black-Eyed Peas
☐ Collard Greens
☐ Mashed Potatoes
☐ Fresh Peach Pie with Vanilla Ice Cream

CAJUN FRIED CHICKEN WITH PECAN GRAVY

■────────────────────────────────────■

One 2½- to 4-pound frying
   chicken, cut up
2 to 3 tablespoons Cajun spice mix,
   any brand or homemade

½ cup all-purpose flour
¼ cup vegetable oil

HOMEMADE CAJUN SPICE MIX:
1 tablespoon chili powder
1 teaspoon paprika
½ teaspoon each ground black

pepper, salt, cayenne pepper,
and dried thyme

1. Place the chicken pieces on a large platter or cake pan. Sprinkle half the Cajun spice mix on one side, turn the pieces and sprinkle the other side. Cover and let rest at least 15 minutes.

2. Dredge the chicken in the flour, shaking the pieces to remove any excess.

3. Place your largest, heaviest frying pan over medium-high heat. Add the vegetable oil and heat for 1 minute. Fry the chicken in the oil until golden

36

brown, 8 to 10 minutes. Remove the chicken pieces from the pan and keep warm.

FOR THE GRAVY:

4 scallions, including green parts, chopped

½ teaspoon cracked black pepper

⅔ cup chopped pecans

¼ cup all-purpose flour

1½ to 2 cups milk

1. Return the same pan to the burner and lower heat to medium. Add the scallions to the oil remaining in the pan and fry for 2 minutes. Add the pepper and pecan halves. Fry for 2 minutes more. Add the flour and fry for 2 minutes, stirring to mix the flour and oil to form a roux.

2. Slowly add the milk to the pan and stir to make gravy. Cook for 5 minutes, adding more milk if necessary to make a smooth, creamy gravy. Cover and keep warm.

BLACK-EYED PEAS

4 strips thick-cut smoky bacon, chopped

2 stalks celery, chopped

½ green bell pepper, seeded and chopped

1 medium onion, peeled and chopped

1½ cups black-eyed peas

½ teaspoon each salt and black pepper

1. Place the bacon in a 3- to 4-quart saucepan. Turn the heat to medium and fry the bacon 3 minutes until it starts to crisp. Add the celery, bell pepper, and onion. Fry another 3 to 5 minutes until the vegetables are soft.

2. Add the black-eyed peas, 3 cups water, salt, and pepper. Turn the heat to high and bring the water to a boil. Cover the pot, reduce heat to low, and simmer for 15 minutes, or until the peas are tender but still firm.

3. Using a potato masher or wire whisk, mash the peas in the pot with 10 firm strokes of the tool. This will make the proper blend of mashed and unmashed peas. Stir the peas over low heat for 2 to 3 minutes. The peas should be thick, like a stew, but still quite moist. Keep warm.

COLLARD GREENS

1 bunch collard, turnip, or mustard
   greens

4 strips thick-cut bacon
1/4 teaspoon each salt and pepper

1. Wash and chop the greens, removing any stems or damaged parts. Drain and set aside.

2. Chop the bacon across the grain into 1/2-inch strips. Place in a pot large enough to hold the chopped greens. Sauté the bacon over medium heat until crispy. Drain all but 2 tablespoons of the bacon drippings.

3. Add the chopped greens to the pot, along with the salt and pepper. Stir the greens in the hot bacon drippings to coat. Add 1 cup water, bring to a boil, reduce heat to medium, and cover the pot. Simmer for 20 to 25 minutes. This will produce crunchy, not soggy, greens.

MASHED POTATOES

6 medium-sized white all-purpose
   potatoes
2 tablespoons butter

1/2 to 3/4 cup milk
Salt and freshly ground pepper to
   taste

1. Wash and peel the potatoes. Quarter them. Put them in a saucepan with 3 cups water. Bring to a boil and cook 10 minutes, or until the potatoes are cooked through but still firm. Drain and return to the pan.

2. Add the butter and the milk to the pan with the potatoes. Use a potato masher or sturdy wire whisk and mash the potatoes to desired consistency, lumpy or creamy. Add salt and pepper to taste. Cover and keep warm.

FRESH PEACH PIE

CRUST:

2 cups all-purpose flour

1 teaspoon salt

⅔ cup cold shortening, either
butter, margarine, or Crisco

1. Sift the flour and the salt in a bowl. Add the shortening. Using two knives or a pastry cutter, work the shortening and the flour together until the mixture becomes grainy and coarse. Add ¼ cup cold water and form the mixture into a ball. Wrap in wax paper and refrigerate 30 minutes.

2. Remove the mixture from the refrigerator and cut it in half. Sprinkle a handful of flour on the countertop and keep another handful nearby. Rub flour on the rolling pin and on the pie dough and roll out each half to form two 11-inch-diameter circles. Keeping everything lightly dusted with flour helps the rolling process.

3. Line a 9-inch pie plate with one circle of pastry. Fill the pie and place the other circle on top. Pinch the edges of the two crusts together decoratively and prick the top crust with a fork.

PEACH FILLING:

4 cups sliced fresh peaches

1 egg, beaten

1 tablespoon all-purpose flour

¾ cup granulated sugar

1. Preheat the oven to 425°F. Place the peaches in a large bowl. In a separate small bowl, stir together the egg, flour, and sugar. Add to the peaches and stir.

2. Pour the peach mixture into the pie crust, cover with top crust, place the pie in the oven, and bake for 10 minutes. Reduce heat to 350°F. and continue baking for 30 minutes longer. Remove from oven and cool before serving.

Make the pie first so that it has time to cool. Next prepare the black-eyed peas because they can cool down on the back of the stove and then be reheated, which improves their flavor.

Put the collard greens in the pot with the bacon and start cooking them.

Sprinkle the Cajun spices on the chicken, dredge the pieces in the flour, and start frying the chicken. While you are frying the chicken, put the potatoes on to boil.

When the last piece of chicken is fried, make the pecan gravy. Mash the potatoes, reheat the peas and greens, and start serving.

BEVERAGES. I think ice-cold beer in long-neck bottles is the thing to drink with this kind of food. Try to get Dixie, brewed in New Orleans, or Lone Star or Shiner from Texas, although Corona or Carta Blanca from Mexico would be good also. Or if you have a beer brewed locally, drink that. No highfalutin' beers for this meal.

Iced tea is the best drink for those who don't want alcohol.

AMBIENCE. Think jukebox honky-tonk for this meal. Commander Cody and His Lost Planet Airmen, Hank Williams, Carl Perkins, and some early Elvis would be good, too. Bob Wills and his Texas Playboys, Dwight Yokum, Waylon Jennings, Johnny Cash, and Willie Nelson also make music to fit this mood.

For the table I would use mismatched white dinerware with little flower patterns, a checkered tablecloth, and a set of fifties tourist salt and pepper shakers that your parents picked up on their trip to Lookout Mountain in Chattanooga.

A flashing neon sign that reads "Eats" would add color, as would some posters of 16-wheelers, or calendars from auto parts dealers.

Mexican Seafood ■

Food in Mexico is a lot more than beans and tortillas.

SERVES 4

☐ Seviche of Sea Scallops and Fresh Tuna
☐ Red Snapper La Ventosa
☐ Arroz Amarillo—Yellow rice
☐ Warm Tortillas
☐ Fresh Mango Slices

SEVICHE OF SEA SCALLOPS AND FRESH TUNA

3/4 pound large fresh sea scallops
1/4 pound fresh tuna
Juice of 6 limes
1/4 cup olive oil
1 medium-sized red ripe tomato, cored and chopped fine
2 fresh serrano or jalapeño peppers, seeded and thinly sliced
1/2 cup red or green bell peppers, seeded and chopped fine

1/2 medium-sized red onion, peeled and sliced very thin
2 cloves garlic, peeled and minced
1/4 cup minced fresh parsley
1/2 teaspoon dried oregano
Salt and pepper to taste
2 cups thinly sliced lettuce leaves

1. Slice the scallops across the grain into thin disks. Slice the tuna into thin strips. Place both in a bowl and cover with the squeezed juice of the limes. Cover and refrigerate the fish for 5 to 6 hours, or overnight. The acid in the lime juice "cooks" the fish and changes it from raw to edible.

2. Drain the lime juice from the fish. Add the olive oil to the lime juice and whisk to make a creamy dressing. Add the tomato, peppers, onion, garlic, parsley, oregano, salt, and pepper. Stir. Add the scallops and tuna and stir, making sure all the vegetables and fish are covered with the dressing.

41

3. Make a bed of chopped lettuce on four individual salad plates. Spoon the seviche on the lettuce and serve.

RED SNAPPER LA VENTOSA

2 pounds red snapper fillets, cut in serving portions

1 medium onion, peeled and minced

3 cloves garlic, peeled and minced

3 tablespoons olive or other vegetable oil

2 fresh jalapeño peppers, seeded and sliced fine

1 green or red bell pepper, cored, seeded, and chopped

2 tomatillos, husks removed, chopped

1 small lime, halved and sliced thin

1/2 cup chopped fresh cilantro

1/4 cup chopped fresh parsley

One 28-ounce can plum tomatoes in sauce, or 4 cups chopped fresh tomatoes

Salt and pepper to taste

1. Wash the fillets, drain them well, and put them in the refrigerator, covered.

2. Sauté the onion and garlic in olive oil over medium-high heat for 3 minutes. Add the peppers and tomatillos and sauté another 2 minutes. Add the lime, cilantro, parsley, tomatoes, salt, and pepper. Bring to a boil, reduce heat to low, and simmer, covered, for 15 to 20 minutes, stirring and adding water if the mixture becomes too thick.

3. Place the snapper fillets in a lidded skillet, pot, or fish poacher large enough to hold them flat in 1 layer. Pour the sauce over the fish and cook over medium heat (do not boil) for 7 minutes. Turn off the heat and let rest until ready to serve.

ARROZ AMARILLO

1½ cups white rice
2 tablespoons butter

½ teaspoon paprika

    1. Sauté the rice in the butter over medium heat for 5 minutes, stirring often, until the rice has turned a golden color. Add the paprika and 3 cups water. Bring the rice to a boil, cover, turn the heat to very low, and cook for 10 to 12 minutes.
    2. Turn off the heat and let the rice rest for 10 minutes. Remove the lid, stir with a fork, and return the lid until ready to serve.

MANGO SLICES

2 large ripe mangoes
½ teaspoon granulated sugar

Juice of ½ lemon
⅛ teaspoon ground cinnamon

    1. Peel and slice the mangoes into bite-sized pieces. Place them in an attractive glass serving bowl. Add the sugar, lemon juice, and cinnamon. Stir, cover, and refrigerate for up to 2 hours before serving.

The scallops and tuna need to marinate in the lime juice for several hours, but once that is done, everything else can be prepared in less than an hour.

Drain the scallops and tuna, make the dressing, mix everything together and let marinate while making everything else. Make the tomato sauce for the red snapper. Slice the mangoes. Put the rice on to cook.

When the rice is finished, put the snapper fillets in the sauce and cook. Serve the seviche. Serve the rice and snapper. Serve the mangoes.

BEVERAGES. Ice-cold Mexican beer is the obvious choice for this meal. Sol and Corona Extra are the most like American beer, Superior and Bohemia are golden, with a bit more flavor, and Dos Equis is a brown beer that is delicious.

Down on the Pacific coast of Mexico they love to serve fresh green coconuts that are hacked open with a machete and spiked with tequila or mescal. Green coconuts can be found in Caribbean, Mexican, and Latin American groceries. Hack and slice off one side of the coconut as if you are making spiked watermelon. Add 1½ ounces tequila or mescal to the coconut milk inside and sip through a straw. Gringos call these coco loco.

If you really want to serve wine, pour a well-chilled German or German-style wine like Gewürztraminer or Riesling, or French Muscadet.

AMBIENCE. I learned to make this red snapper quite by accident while camping on the beach south of Salina Cruz in the Bay of Tehuantepec. We bought fish, actually Sierra or Spanish mackerel, from a boy on the beach. We had bought vegetables and hot peppers at the market, so we just cooked what we had, including the limes.

La Vista Hermosa, the restaurant where I spent a lot of time in La Ventosa, was a large open-air pulapa made of felled coconut trees and palm leaves. The people who worked there simply slept in the hammocks that were lifted to the ceiling during the day. To re-create something like this, rent or borrow a few palm plants and drape a colorful hammock along one wall. Put some plastic iguanas or lizards around the room.

Every night a pickup truck carrying a mariachi band with a huge xylophone would pull up to La Vista Hermosa and make music. Buy some mariachi records and some mariachi shakers and sing along.

Mexican Seafood

■ Provençal ■

The smells and flavors of Provence are as memorable as the light.

SERVES 4

- ☐ Pissaladière—Niçoise pizza
- ☐ Monkfish Marseilles
- ☐ Buttered Rice
- ☐ Salade Soleil
- ☐ Fresh Fruit in Season

PISSALADIÈRE

FOR THE DOUGH:

1 loaf frozen bread dough or:
1 package yeast
1 tablespoon granulated sugar

4 cups all-purpose flour
¼ teaspoon salt
2 tablespoons olive oil

THE TOPPING:

3 medium or 2 large red onions, peeled and sliced very thin
3 tablespoons olive oil
1 small tin or jar best-quality anchovy fillets

2 tablespoons chopped fresh rosemary leaves
3 tablespoons tiny black Niçoise olives

1. Let the frozen bread dough thaw and rise according to package instructions. Or make the dough: Mix the yeast in a medium-sized bowl with 1 cup lukewarm water and the sugar. Stir and let rest 5 minutes.

2. Add the flour, salt, and olive oil to the yeast mixture, stirring to form a ball of dough. Knead the dough for 5 to 10 minutes until it is smooth and elastic. Place in a clean bowl, cover with a towel, and let rise in a warm place for 1 hour. Punch down the dough and let rise another hour. Roll dough onto a pizza pan and let rest 5 minutes.

46

4. For the topping, sauté the onions with the olive oil in a skillet

over medium-high heat 5 to 7 minutes, or until onions are soft and slightly brown.

5. Preheat the oven to 500°F. Place the onion topping on the pizza dough. Lay 6 to 10 anchovy fillets, depending on preference, on top of the onions. Sprinkle on the rosemary leaves and the olives. Bake in the hot oven 10 to 15 minutes, or until the crust is golden brown.

MONKFISH MARSEILLES

4 fillets monkfish or other firm-fleshed white fish such as cod or red snapper	1 bay leaf
	1 teaspoon dried tarragon
	6 to 8 saffron threads
3 tablespoons olive oil	1/2 teaspoon crushed fennel seeds
1 medium onion, peeled and chopped fine	One 28-ounce can Italian plum tomatoes
3 cloves garlic, peeled and chopped fine	1/2 cup minced fresh parsley
	Salt and pepper to taste
2 medium shallots, peeled and chopped fine	

1. Wash and dry the fillets and set them aside.

2. Make the sauce in a large saucepan. Sauté the onion in the olive oil over medium-high heat for 3 minutes, stirring often. Add the garlic and shallots and lower the heat to medium. Sauté for 5 minutes.

3. Add the remaining ingredients, stirring carefully and breaking the tomatoes into smaller pieces. Bring to a boil, reduce heat to medium-low, cover, and simmer for 20 minutes.

4. Preheat the oven to 425°F. Place the fish fillets in an ovenproof glass, pottery, or stainless-steel casserole dish. Pour the sauce over and bake the fish in the oven for 10 minutes.

BUTTERED RICE

2 tablespoons butter   1 cup long-grain white rice

1. Sauté the rice in the butter over medium heat for 3 to 5 minutes, stirring often until the rice turns a golden brown.

2. Pour 1¾ cups water over the rice and bring the mixture to the boil. Cover the saucepan, reduce the heat to very low, and let cook 10 minutes. During that time do not stir and do not lift the lid. Turn off the heat and let rest for 10 minutes. Fluff with a fork.

SALADE SOLEIL

1 head red or green leaf lettuce   Pinch of salt and freshly ground
1 tablespoon lemon juice   black pepper
3 tablespoons French olive oil

1. Wash, drain, and dry lettuce leaves. Break into bite-sized pieces and reserve.

2. Pour the lemon juice into the bottom of a large wooden salad bowl. Add the olive oil, salt, and pepper. Whisk to make a creamy dressing.

3. Place the lettuce leaves in the bowl and toss with the dressing.

FRESH FRUIT IN SEASON

After all the tangy flavors here, your palate is going to need a very simple dessert. I suggest whatever fruit is in season at the time. Sliced peaches, melon, even a crisp apple will taste good at the end of this meal.

Start working on the pizza dough first. If you are using frozen dough, you have to thaw it out several hours ahead of time. If you are making your own dough, budget 2 hours for kneading and letting the dough rise.

While the dough is rising you can make the sauce for the monkfish. You can also start frying the onions for the pissaladière. Wash and dry the lettuce, wrap it in paper towels, and place it in the refrigerator.

Your guests have arrived and you are in the final stretch. Preheat the oven to 500°F. Spread the pizza dough over your pizza pan. Put on the toppings and bake. Put the rice on to cook.

Put the monkfish in the baking dish and pour on the sauce. When the pizza comes out of the oven, reduce the heat to 425°F. and put the monkfish in the oven. Take the rice off the heat and let it rest. Serve the pissaladière.

Return to the kitchen. Remove the monkfish from the oven. Place fish, sauce, and rice on individual plates and serve.

Return to the kitchen. Make the salad dressing and toss with the lettuce. Serve.

Serve the dessert.

BEVERAGES. This meal reflects the cuisine of Avignon to Provence, the maritime region of the south of France that stretches from Marseilles to Nice. To be authentic, you should drink a dry rosé wine from the area but these can be difficult to find in the United States. A good alternative would be the dry, light, white zinfandels of California. Another option would be a dry rosé of Portugal, such as Mateus.

AMBIENCE. This meal features the food of the Riviera. A good theme would be a Riviera party with yachts, discotheques, and that aura of the spoiled European rich kids known as Eurotrash.

But a better idea would be to capitalize on the color of the two main cities represented in the menu, Nice and Marseilles. Nice is close to the Italian border and the pissaladière is an Italian-influenced French pizza. Nice was home to the great artist Henri Matisse. Pablo Picasso lived in nearby Golfe Juan. The original Chez Panisse was a Marseilles waterfront bar featured in the novels of Marcel Pagnol.

So the theme for your party is to have Picasso and Matisse come to dinner at Chez Panisse in Marseilles. Get some Picasso and Matisse posters from the library. Since Maurice Chevalier played Panisse in *Fanny*, a movie based on the work of Pagnol, get some of his recordings for music.

The table setting should be casual and relaxed. Instead of flowers, get tiny pots of lavender, rosemary, or thyme, the herbs of Provence.

■ French Bistro ■

And afterward, smoke yellow Gauloises and discuss existentialism,
or sing the Marseillaise.

SERVES 4

☐ Cream of Leek Soup with Fresh Herbs
☐ Roast Chicken with Tarragon
☐ Stuffed Tomatoes
☐ Baked Apples with Calvados

CREAM OF LEEK SOUP WITH FRESH HERBS

4 leeks, white parts only, washed
    and thinly sliced
4 medium-sized white potatoes,
    peeled
2 tablespoons unsalted butter
1 quart chicken stock, homemade
    or canned

1 pint half-and-half
1 tablespoon each minced fresh
    chives, parsley, and chervil
Salt and freshly ground black
    pepper to taste

1. Wash the leeks carefully because there can be sand hidden in their many layers of leaves. Quarter the potatoes.

2. In a 4-quart soup pot, sauté the leeks in the butter over medium heat for 3 minutes. Add the potatoes and chicken stock. Bring to a boil, turn the heat to medium, cover, and simmer for 20 minutes. Turn off the heat and cool for 5 minutes.

3. Purée the leeks, potatoes, and chicken stock in a food processor. Return the purée to the soup pot and add the half-and-half, three-quarters of the herbs, salt, and pepper. Simmer over low heat for 10 minutes. Do not boil.

4. Serve the soup in bowls and sprinkle the remaining herbs on top.

51

ROAST CHICKEN WITH TARRAGON

One 3- to 5-pound roasting chicken
3 tablespoons fresh or 1 tablespoon
 dried tarragon leaves
2 cloves garlic, peeled and minced
2 tablespoons unsalted butter,
 softened

1/2 teaspoon salt
1/4 teaspoon freshly ground black
 pepper
1/2 cup white wine

1. Preheat the oven to 350°F. Remove the giblets from the bird and save for another use. Wash and dry the bird and place it in a large, low-sided roasting pan.

2. Mash the tarragon with the garlic, butter, salt, and pepper. Rub two-thirds of this mixture on the outside of the bird and rub the remainder around the inside of the cavity.

3. Place the bird in the oven, breast side down, and bake for 18 to 20 minutes per pound. That's 1 hour to 1 hour and 40 minutes, depending on the size of the bird.

4. Halfway through the roasting time, turn the bird breast side up and continue to roast. Oven temperatures vary widely. The chicken is done when the leg wiggles easily and when the juices from the leg run clear when pierced with a fork.

5. Remove the bird from the oven and loosely wrap with foil. Let the chicken rest for 10 to 15 minutes before you carve it.

6. Make a pan juice sauce. Tilt the pan and skim the fat from the juices. Deglaze the pan by placing it over medium-high heat and adding 1/2 cup of white wine or water. Stir often and let the juices bubble and thicken. Pour sauce into a bowl and serve with the chicken.

STUFFED TOMATOES

4 large ripe red tomatoes
1 cup finely chopped French
    bread crumbs
½ cup minced fresh parsley
3 tablespoons olive oil

1 clove garlic, peeled and minced
3 tablespoons grated Parmesan
    cheese
¼ teaspoon freshly ground black
    pepper

1. Cut the tomatoes in half and scoop the pulp and juice into a medium-sized bowl.

2. Add the bread crumbs, parsley, olive oil, garlic, Parmesan cheese, and pepper to the pulp. Stir and let rest for 10 minutes, enough time for the bread to soak up the juices and flavors.

3. Preheat the oven to 375°F. Stuff the tomato halves with the bread mixture, place them in an ovenproof casserole dish, and bake them in the oven for 10 minutes. Then place them under the broiler, 6 inches from the heat source, for 1 to 2 minutes, or until they brown on top.

BAKED APPLES WITH CALVADOS

4 large golden apples
Juice of ½ lemon
2 tablespoons unsalted butter
2 tablespoons light brown sugar

¼ cup Calvados, Armagnac,
    Cognac, or brandy
½ teaspoon ground cinnamon

1. Core the apples, leaving them whole. Sprinkle with lemon juice and set in a gratin dish or ovenproof casserole.

2. Preheat the oven to 375°F. In a small bowl, mix together the butter, sugar, and Calvados. Spoon the mixture into the holes left by the removed cores. Sprinkle the cinnamon over the apples and bake for 30 minutes, or until they can be pierced with a knife.

The first thing you want to do is prepare the bird. Rub it with the butter and herbs and place it in the preheated oven. Check the oven temperature with an oven thermometer available at any housewares store.

While the bird is roasting, make the soup. Cook the vegetables and purée them. Then wait a bit.

Next make the stuffing and fill the tomatoes. Cover and leave at room temperature.

Prepare the apples but don't put them in the oven yet. Cover.

You want your guests' arrival to coincide with the time when you pull the bird from the oven. Put the bird on the carving platter and cover it. Make the pan juice sauce, transfer it from the roasting pan to a small saucepan, cover, and keep warm. Turn the oven to 375°F.

Return to the soup. Place the purée, seasonings, and cream in the soup pot. Heat to hot but not bubbling and serve. Place the tomatoes and the apples in the oven as you leave the kitchen.

Return to the kitchen. Remove the tomatoes from the oven. Carve the chicken and place it on a large platter. Reheat the sauce and place it in a gravy boat with a ladle.

Turn the oven to broil and broil the tomatoes for 1 minute. This short time won't hurt the apples. Remember to turn the oven back down to 375°F. when you remove the tomatoes. Place the tomatoes on the chicken serving platter and serve.

Return to the kitchen, remove the apples, and serve.

BEVERAGES. French wine is what you would serve at a French bistro dinner, either a full-bodied white or a light red. For the white wine I would serve a good-quality Chablis, Macon, or Macon-Villages. You might want to splurge and get a Pouilly-Fuissé or a Meursault.

For a red wine, you might want to try some of the lighter red wines from the Côtes-du-Rhône, the nearby Côtes du Ventoux, or a cru Beaujolais such as Morgon, Moulin-à-Vent, or Chénas.

Bistros in France, especially those that are family-operated, pride themselves on a wine list that features lesser wines from Burgundy and Bordeaux.

These wines are very good, but since they are not as well known, they cost a lot less. Have your trusted wine merchant suggest one of them for you.

AMBIENCE. A French bistro is usually a small unpretentious restaurant, often family-run, with a few tables and a bar. People come there for simple food, well prepared.

Cozy is the operative word when setting a theme for a French bistro dinner. Snug is a good word, too. You want your guests to eat and drink heartily, rub elbows, and maybe get a little boisterous.

White butcher paper is the most common tablecloth at bistros in Paris. The waiters tally the bill right on the paper at the end of the meal. I like those pale blue bistro plates and bowls. I wouldn't put any flowers on the table. Make everything very plain and simple.

Music is whatever you like.

■ Summer Barbecue ■

*It's just as easy as hamburgers and hot dogs, but your friends
will really appreciate something different.*

SERVES 6 TO 8

☐ Fresh Corn and Shrimp Salad
☐ Butterflied Leg of Lamb
☐ Couscous Salad
☐ Blueberry Buckle

FRESH CORN AND SHRIMP SALAD

1 pound medium shrimp, shells on
6 ears fresh corn
1 red bell pepper, cored, seeded,
    and diced
1 green bell pepper, cored, seeded,
    and diced
1 small red onion, peeled and
    minced

1 cup minced fresh cilantro
1/3 cup freshly squeezed lemon
    juice
1 cup olive oil
Salt and pepper to taste

1. Bring 2 quarts of water to a boil in a large pot. Add the shrimp, turn off the heat, cover, and let rest 10 minutes. Remove the shrimp with a slotted spoon and let cool. Peel and reserve shrimp.

2. Pull the husks and silks from the corn. Using a sharp knife, slice the kernels from the cob. Boil the same water you cooked the shrimp in, add the corn, turn off the heat, cover, and let rest 3 minutes. Drain the corn in a colander and run under cold water to stop the cooking process. Drain and reserve.

3. Place the peeled shrimp, corn, red and green bell peppers, onion, and cilantro in a large salad bowl. Stir.

4. In a smaller mixing bowl, place the lemon juice, olive oil, salt, and pepper. Whisk to form a creamy dressing. Add to the shrimp-and-corn mixture. Stir. Cover bowl with plastic wrap and place in the refrigerator for at least 30 minutes for the flavors to mingle.

BUTTERFLIED LEG OF LAMB

1 leg of lamb, about 5 pounds,
    boned and butterflied by the
    butcher
1/2 cup olive oil
3 cloves garlic, peeled and minced

1 tablespoon each dried oregano,
    thyme, and rosemary
1 teaspoon each salt and black
    pepper

1. Place the leg of lamb in a large roasting pan. Rub it well with the olive oil and garlic. Mix the herbs, salt, and pepper together in a small bowl and sprinkle them all over the lamb. Cover and let rest in the refrigerator overnight, or at room temperature for 1 hour.

2. Build a fire in a Weber-type hooded barbecue grill. If you are using a gas grill, turn it on very low.

3. When the coals are an ashen gray or the gas grill is evenly heated at low, place the lamb in the grill about 5 inches from the heat. Cover and roast for 15 minutes. Turn and roast another 15 minutes.

4. A butterflied leg of lamb will have uneven thick and thin parts. When the thickest part is still very blood-rare, pull the meat from the grill. Put the meat on a platter, cover it with foil, and let rest for 15 minutes. The meat will continue to cook during this time, turning blood-rare into perfectly rare. Now you have rare, medium, and well-done pieces to please your guests' tastes. Pour any juices that collected on the platter over the meat and serve.

COUSCOUS SALAD

1 cup couscous (Moroccan semolina pasta)
3/4 cup raisins, dried currants, or sultanas
2 tablespoons butter
3/4 cup chopped celery
3/4 cup grated carrots

1/2 cup pignoli nuts, sliced almonds, or unsalted sunflower seeds
1 teaspoon dried mint
1/2 teaspoon ground cumin
Juice of 1 lemon
1 cup low-fat plain yogurt
Salt and pepper to taste

1. Bring 1 1/2 cups water to a boil and add the couscous. Turn off the heat, cover the pot, and let rest 10 minutes. Fluff the couscous with a fork and place it in a large mixing bowl.

2. Soak the raisins in 1 cup warm water for 10 minutes. Drain them and add to the couscous.

3. Melt the butter over medium-high heat in a frying pan and sauté the celery, carrots, and nuts for 5 minutes, stirring often. Add to the couscous.

5. Add the remaining ingredients to the couscous, stir, cover, and refrigerate for at least 30 minutes for the flavors to mingle.

BLUEBERRY BUCKLE

4 cups fresh blueberries, about 2 pints
1 1/2 cups plus 1 tablespoon all-purpose flour

1 1/2 cups white or light brown sugar
1/2 teaspoon ground cinnamon
1 stick (1/2 cup) unsalted butter

1. Preheat the oven to 350°F. Wash and clean the blueberries of any stems or sticks. Place berries in an 8-by-8-inch casserole or baking pan. Sprinkle 1 tablespoon of flour over the berries and stir to blend.

2. In a mixing bowl, blend 1 1/2 cups flour, sugar, cinnamon, and butter. Crumble the mixture with a fork or your fingertips to form a coarse meal. Spread the mixture over the blueberries and bake for 40 to 45 minutes. Cool and serve.

The secret to this dinner is to have all the indoor cooking done before your guests arrive so that you can spend all of your time with them outdoors.

Marinate the lamb in the large pan with all the ingredients. Remember to turn it over every once in a while so that all sides are exposed to the marinade.

Make the corn and shrimp salad, the couscous salad, and the blueberry buckle. These are very simple recipes and it is best to do them one at a time. Cover the salads and refrigerate. Let the buckle cool and keep it away from people who want just one nibble.

You should probably plan to put the lamb on the barbecue grill shortly after your guests arrive. Start the grill 30 minutes to 1 hour beforehand.

If you are in the country, you can easily make the best barbecue fire of your life with fallen limbs and kindling wood. Open all the vents on your cooker and set the lid to the side. Place two big handfuls of newspaper in the cooker and cover with progressively larger twigs and branches. Light the paper and let the fire burn. Add more sticks to the fire so that you get a 3- to 4-inch bed of wood coals. You will need a bushel basket full of 1- to 2-inch-thick sticks for this fire. Otherwise just use charcoal.

When the fire is ready, place the lamb on the wire rack and put the lid on the cooker. Adjust the vents to half closed. Follow the instructions for cooking the meat, let rest, and carve.

Place the salads on the table while the meat is resting. Serve everything family style.

BEVERAGES. A summer barbecue needs a big cooler filled with cracked ice and the wine, beer, seltzer, and soft drinks of your choice. Get some of the natural sodas like Snapple, Soho, or Natural-90.

Good summer white wines are Italian Soave or Frascati, French white Bordeaux, or California Sauvignon Blanc.

Summer reds should be chillable, so get Beaujolais.

AMBIENCE. I see this as a sunset barbecue. You need a picnic table or large outdoor wooden table, but a folding table with a checkered tablecloth will do.

Use plastic or paper plates; some of them can be quite attractive. Buy paper napkins and flatware to match.

String a set of Japanese lanterns around the yard for a colorful backdrop. Candles won't work in the windy air, but kerosene lamps with good-smelling fluid will do a great job of lighting the table.

Let the sounds of the night be your musical entertainment.

Barbacoa Fajitas ■

A TEX-MEX SOUTHWESTERN BARBECUE

You can make this year round, but the meat tastes so much better when it's cooked outdoors.

SERVES 6 TO 8

- [ ] Flour Tortillas (2 dozen)
- [ ] Mesquite-Grilled Skirt Steak
- [ ] Sweet Corn with Lime-Cilantro Butter
- [ ] Guacamole
- [ ] Salsa Fresca
- [ ] Salsa Verde

MESQUITE-GRILLED SKIRT STEAK

3 pounds skirt steak, London broil, or sirloin
7 limes
6 garlic cloves, peeled and minced
1 teaspoon salt

Freshly ground black pepper to taste
1 teaspoon chili powder
2 tablespoons corn oil or vegetable oil

1. Place the steak in a large shallow bowl. Squeeze the juice of the limes over the steak. Add the garlic, salt, black pepper, chili powder, and vegetable oil. Rub the ingredients into the steak, turning the meat several times to incorporate the marinade. Cover and let rest at room temperature 1 to 2 hours or in the refrigerator overnight.

2. Build a fire in the outdoor grill you intend to use. (If using an indoor broiler, preheat it.) Soak the mesquite or other wood chips in a bucket of water for 1 hour. When the coals are ashen gray, add the drained wood chips to the fire.

3. Place the steak on a grill or a wire rack 4 to 6 inches above the coals.

61

Grill the steak 8 to 10 minutes on each side. Keep it on the rare side for good flavor.

4. Remove steak from grill, cover with foil, and let rest 10 minutes. When it is time to serve, slice the steak across the grain into ¼-inch-thick slices. Keep warm.

SWEET CORN
WITH LIME-CILANTRO BUTTER

8 to 10 ears fresh sweet corn
4 tablespoons (½ stick) unsalted
    butter
1 fresh jalapeño or serrano chili,
    stemmed, seeded, and minced

Juice of 2 limes
½ cup minced fresh cilantro
½ teaspoon freshly ground black
    pepper
¼ teaspoon salt

1. Pull the silk and inner leaves away from the corn and discard, but leave the outer leaves attached.

2. Melt the butter over low heat. Add the fresh green chili peppers, the lime juice, cilantro, pepper, and salt. Stir and continue cooking for 3 minutes.

3. Brush the corn with the lime-cilantro butter. Reclose the outer husks around the ears of corn. Twist the ends to make a tight wrap. Use a twisty or a piece of string if necessary to enclose the corn tightly.

4. Roast the corn on the grill after you have removed the steak. Cover the grill with a domed lid or a sheet of heavy aluminum foil to keep the heat in. Roast for 5 minutes, turn the corn, and roast for another 5 minutes. Serve the corn in its husks.

GUACAMOLE

2 whole ripe avocados
5 fresh or pickled jalapeño peppers,
    seeded and minced
1 ripe fresh tomato, cored and
    diced fine
2 tablespoons minced fresh
    cilantro

1 small onion, peeled and minced
Juice of 1 lemon and 1 lime
2 tablespoons good mayonnaise
1 teaspoon chili powder

1. Peel and seed the avocados. Mash in a medium-sized bowl. Add the minced peppers, tomato, cilantro, onion, juices, mayonnaise, and chili powder. Mash with a potato masher or a heavy wire whisk. Stir and keep tightly covered.

SALSA FRESCA

1 pound fresh tomatoes or one
    28-ounce can, peeled, seeded,
    and chopped
3 fresh or canned serrano or
    jalapeño chilis, seeded and
    chopped

1 medium onion, peeled and
    chopped
2 tablespoons chopped fresh
    cilantro
Juice of 1 lemon
2 cloves garlic, peeled and chopped

1. Place all ingredients in a blender or food processor and blend to a smooth sauce, 2 to 3 quick pulses for a processor and 30 seconds for a blender.

SALSA VERDE

4 to 5 fresh whole husked or 1 cup
    drained canned tomatillos,
    chopped
1 small onion, peeled and chopped

2 small jalapeño or serrano chilis,
    seeded and chopped
2 tablespoons chopped fresh
    cilantro

1. Place all ingredients in a blender or food processor and blend to a smooth sauce, 2 to 3 quick pulses for a processor and 30 seconds for a blender.

The first thing you have to do is to marinate the steak—the longer the better. But if you are pressed for time, at least marinate the steak before you light the barbecue fire.

Once the fire is going, you can make the salsa fresca and salsa verde. While the coals are getting ready, assemble the ingredients for the guacamole.

When your guests start arriving, barbecue the steak and corn. Keep them warm. Warm the flour tortillas by wrapping them in a double thickness of aluminum foil and place them over the hot coals, or in the oven for 7 minutes.

Slice the steak. Put the sauces in colorful ceramic bowls. Arrange the corn on a large platter. Keep the tortillas in foil. At the very last minute, when everyone is assembled to eat, make the guacamole with a grand flourish.

Let your guests serve themselves by making their own fajitas out of the ingredients: Hold the warm tortilla in one hand. Place a small amount of the steak on the tortilla. Put a spoonful of guacamole on that and a spoonful of either salsa fresca or salsa verde on that. Roll and eat.

DESSERT. Watermelon, preferably the yellow Hopi watermelon or Southwestern watermelon, is perfect. But feel free to substitute any other tropical fruit such as mango or papaya.

BEVERAGES. A number of good-tasting and available Mexican beers would be perfect for this barbacoa. Bohemia is my first choice, followed by Dos Equis. Then try Superior and Corona. Margaritas are the first choice in mixed drinks.

Margaritas: Fill blender half full with crushed ice. Add 4 ounces tequila or mescal, 2 ounces triple sec, 6 ounces sweet-and-sour mix. Blend till smooth. (Makes 1 quart.) Serve drinks with lime wedges. Skip the salt.

AMBIENCE. What you're going for here is an outdoor, backyard barbecue with a Tex-Mex Southwestern flavor, the kind they have in the border country around the Rio Grande, what Mexicans call the Rio Bravo. Down in this country there are conjunto bands, traveling groups of players that carry guitars, accordions, and maybe trumpets from party to party. Records of this music are available at record stores. Records by Los Lobos of "La Bamba" fame are much more widely available.

Set the table with as much stone pottery as you have. A cactus is good. Fresh and dried chili pepper make a good centerpiece.

Set out a bowl of tortilla chips and some extra salsa fresca and salsa verde for early guests. A bowl of pickled jalapeño peppers is also customary for those who like hot stuff, and a bowl of lime wedges should be provided for tequila, mescal, and beer drinkers.

■ Thai Taste ■

The most sensuous combination of flavors in the world.

SERVES 4

- ☐ Siam Vegetable Salad
- ☐ Chicken Satay with Peanut Butter Sauce
- ☐ Pad Thai—Thai noodles with shrimp
- ☐ Tea and Oranges

SIAM VEGETABLE SALAD

4 large carrots, peeled and sliced
   into thin strips
4 large lettuce leaves, washed and
   dried
1 medium cucumber, peeled and
   sliced into 3-inch spears
1 large green or red bell pepper,
   cored, seeded, and sliced into
   strips
1 medium tomato, sliced into
   wedges
1 medium red onion, peeled and
   sliced into rings

1 cup alfalfa, radish, or mung bean
   sprouts

FOR THE DRESSING:
2 tablespoons nam pla fish sauce
1 tablespoon soy sauce
3 tablespoons lemon juice
1/4 teaspoon each sugar and chili
   sauce
3 tablespoons vegetable oil

1. Drop the carrots sticks into a small saucepan of boiling water. Simmer for 5 minutes and drain. Cool under cold water. Drain.

2. Place the lettuce leaves as a bed on a large flat salad platter. Arrange all the vegetables on the lettuce leaves.

3. Place all the dressing ingredients in a small bowl and whisk to form a smooth dressing. Pour over the vegetables and serve.

67

CHICKEN SATAY
WITH PEANUT BUTTER SAUCE

4 half chicken breasts, boneless
  and skinless

FOR THE MARINADE:
2 cloves garlic, peeled and minced
1 teaspoon minced fresh ginger
2 teaspoons curry powder
1/2 cup coconut milk or cream
2 tablespoons lime juice

FOR THE PEANUT SAUCE:
1/2 cup chunky peanut butter
1/4 cup coconut milk or cream
2 scallions, minced, green tops
  included
1/2 teaspoon hot chili sauce
1 tablespoon lemon or lime juice

1. Cut the chicken breasts into bite-sized chunks.

2. Put all the marinade ingredients in a medium mixing bowl. Stir to blend well. Add the chicken pieces to the marinade, cover, and let rest 1 hour at room temperature or overnight in the refrigerator. Just before broiling thread the pieces equally on 8 wooden satay skewers.

3. Preheat the broiler. Arrange the skewered chicken on a broiler pan and broil 4 to 6 inches from the heat source for 1 to 2 minutes. Turn and broil another 1 to 2 minutes.

4. Place all the peanut sauce ingredients in a saucepan. Cook over medium heat, stirring often, until all the ingredients are combined and hot. Serve with the chicken.

PAD THAI

½ pound Chinese rice vermicelli

4 ounces dried Chinese mushroom caps

1 medium onion, peeled, halved, and sliced thin

3 tablespoons vegetable oil

2 cloves garlic, peeled and minced

2 carrots, coarsely grated to make about 1 cup

½ pound medium shrimp, shells on

1 cup mung bean sprouts

½ cup minced cilantro (Chinese parsley)

3 tablespoons lime juice

2 tablespoons nam pla fish sauce

2 tablespoons crunchy peanut butter

Lettuce leaves, lemon wedges, bean sprouts, cilantro leaves for garnish

1. Soak the rice noodles and mushroom caps in separate bowls in warm water until they are soft and tender, about 20 minutes. Drain and reserve.

2. In a wok, deep-sided skillet, or kettle, sauté the onion in the oil over medium-high heat 3 minutes. Add the garlic, carrots, shrimp in their shells, and bean sprouts. Lower the heat to medium and sauté for 3 minutes, stirring often.

3. Add the cilantro, lime juice, fish sauce, peanut butter, and drained mushrooms to the wok. Stir to mix well. Add the noodles and stir to blend well. Cook over medium heat 3 minutes, stirring.

4. Serve the pad Thai on a large platter garnished with lettuce leaves, lemon wedges, bean sprouts, and cilantro leaves.

One good thing about this meal is that you serve everything at once. Put all the food on the table at the same time and let people help themselves.

Start by combining the ingredients to marinate the chicken. Put the chicken pieces in the mixture and stir.

Soak the vermicelli and the mushroom caps for the pad Thai.

Cook the carrots for the salad and prepare all the remaining vegetables for all the dishes. Put them in separate bowls and keep ready.

Make the Siam vegetable salad but don't put the dressing on. Cover with plastic wrap and place in the refrigerator.

Arrange the chicken pieces on the skewers and make the peanut sauce. When your guests arrive, start making the pad Thai. Turn the broiler on for the chicken satay. Broil the chicken satay, put the satay on a platter, cover, and keep warm. Finish the pad Thai and place on a large platter.

Pour the dressing on the Siam salad, and bring the salad, the satay, and the pad Thai to the table all at once on separate platters.

Make the tea and bring it along with the oranges to the table.

Serve a bowl of hot chili sauce for those who like their food spicy.

BEVERAGES. Singha beer imported from Thailand is the best beverage to go with this meal. Tsingtao from China, or Kirin, Suntory, or any beer from Japan is a good substitute. You could also serve Heineken or Beck's.

If you serve tea, it should be a green Chinese tea.

AMBIENCE. Thailand is a Southeast Asian country like Vietnam or Cambodia. It is hot and it is tropical. You could create an atmosphere like that of the many open-air cafés that are decorated with bamboo screens and curtains, and dressed with brightly colored twinkling lights.

You could make a table setting of bamboo, coconuts, tropical fruits, and hot chili peppers. Bamboo place mats would be good. Naturally you would buy a record or tape of Thai music.

Some of your timid guests may think the combination of flavors in Thai cooking is a little weird. Peanut butter on chicken? Fish sauce on salad? Well, they are weird to American taste buds. Just reassure them that a lot of Americans put ketchup on cottage cheese and that good old Worcestershire sauce is made from fermented anchovies and everybody likes that, right?

■ California Classic ■

With its incorporation of Asian flavors, classical Continental techniques, and American emphasis on freshness and quality ingredients, California cuisine must be the ultimate melting pot.

SERVES 4

- ☐ Warm Goat Cheese Salad on a Bed of Mixed Greens
- ☐ Lobster Fettuccine with Ginger/Cilantro Cream Sauce
- ☐ Tiramisù

WARM GOAT CHEESE SALAD
ON A BED OF MIXED GREENS

■ ━━━━━━━━━━━━━━━━━━━━━━━━━━━━━━━━━━━━ ■

½ pound fresh white goat cheese (chèvre), packaged in a log shape
½ cup unflavored bread crumbs
1 small bunch arugula
2 large heads mâche

1 head red leaf lettuce
3 tablespoons extra virgin olive oil
1 tablespoon raspberry vinegar
Pinch each salt and pepper

1. Refrigerate the chèvre log until it is very cold and firm, about 1 hour. Slice the chèvre into 4 equal disks, each about 1 inch thick. Coat the cheese disks with the bread crumbs, pressing the crumbs into the cheese to form a crust. Refrigerate for 1 hour.

2. Wash and separate the lettuces. Break into bite-sized pieces. Drain and dry with paper towels.

3. In a small mixing bowl, blend the olive oil, vinegar, salt, and pepper, whisking to form a smooth, creamy dressing.

4. Preheat the broiler. Place the bread crumb–coated chèvre disks 4 inches from the heat and toast for 30 seconds. Flip them carefully and toast for another 15 seconds. Remove from the broiler and keep warm.

71

5. Toss the salad greens with the dressing and divide among four individual salad plates. Arrange chèvre disks on top of the greens and serve.

LOBSTER FETTUCCINE
WITH GINGER/CILANTRO CREAM SAUCE

Two 1½- to 2-pound live lobsters
¾ pound fettuccine
½ cup minced scallions, including
    green tops
1 clove garlic, peeled and minced
2 teaspoons minced fresh ginger
3 tablespoons olive oil

½ cup minced fresh cilantro
1 stick (½ cup) unsalted butter
3 medium tomatoes
2 cups heavy cream
¼ teaspoon each salt and freshly
    ground black pepper

1. Bring a large pot of water to the boil. Add the lobsters, cover, and simmer for 5 minutes. Remove lobsters and let them cool.

2. In a large skillet or sauté pan, sauté the scallions, garlic, and ginger in the olive oil over medium heat for 3 minutes, stirring often. Add the cilantro and butter and reduce heat to low to let butter melt.

3. Core the tomatoes and cut them in half. Scoop out the seeds and juice and discard. Finely chop remaining tomato and add to the sauté pan.

4. Remove the lobster meat from the tails and claws. If there is any pink coral, save that, too. Chop the lobster meat into small bite-sized chunks. Add the lobster meat to the sauce and cook over low heat for 1 minute, stirring often.

5. Add the cream and salt and pepper to the sauce and lobster meat. Cook over medium heat until hot but not bubbling, stirring often.

6. Meanwhile, cook the fettuccine in a large pot of boiling water until al dente, or tender but still slightly chewy. Drain and keep warm.

7. Toss the lobster sauce with the fettuccine and serve.

TIRAMISÙ

1 pound ladyfingers or Italian
    ladyfingerlike biscotti
1 cup prepared espresso coffee
1/4 cup dark rum
2 tablespoons Frangelico or
    Amaretto liqueur

1 pound mascarpone or cream
    cheese
6 eggs, separated
1/2 cup granulated sugar
1/4 cup cocoa powder

1. Lay the ladyfingers flat on a large cookie sheet or jelly roll pan with a rim and pour the coffee over them. Pour on the rum and liqueur. Let the liquids soak in for 10 minutes.

2. Place the mascarpone or cream cheese in a large mixing bowl. Add the egg yolks and 6 tablespoons sugar. Beat until smooth.

3. In another bowl, beat the egg whites until firm. Fold the egg whites into the mascarpone mixture.

4. Arrange half the ladyfingers in the bottom of a glass or pottery casserole dish. Spread half the mascarpone mixture over them. Place the remaining ladyfingers on top and cover with the rest of the mascarpone mixture. Cover with plastic wrap and refrigerate for at least 4 hours or, better yet, overnight.

5. Mix the remaining 2 tablespoons sugar with the cocoa powder and sprinkle on the tiramisù just before you serve it.

Make the tiramisù the night before the meal.

Wash and dry the greens for the salad. Make the dressing. Press the bread crumbs into the cheese disks, cover, and refrigerate.

Make the lobster sauce up to the last step before tossing with the noodles. Put the water for the noodles on high heat.

Toss the salad with the dressing. Broil the cheese disks and serve the salad.

Boil the noodles, drain, and keep warm.

Reheat the lobster sauce and toss it with the noodles. Serve.

Sprinkle the cocoa powder on the tiramisù and serve.

BEVERAGES. I would serve two different California wines with this meal. With the chèvre salad I would serve a full-bodied and oaky-flavored California Chardonnay. There are a lot of them out there but Mondavi Reserve, Beringer, Glen Ellen, and Fetzer are labels with wide distribution.

With the lobster fettuccine I would serve a light Cabernet Sauvignon or a light zinfandel. Don't get a big, heavy wine that will overpower the lobster. You want one that will let the flavors come through.

You might use this meal to sample a variety of California wines. You could make notes on the flavor of the wine by itself and in concert with the food.

AMBIENCE. There are at least two Californias. Northern California around San Francisco and the Bay Area is one. And Southern California, centered around Los Angeles is another.

California cuisine, developed by Alice Waters, Jeremiah Tower, and dozens of other chefs, relies on interesting combinations of flavors that cut across ethnic culinary boundaries. But the foundation is usually classical French technique fueled by delicious California food products.

I would present this dinner as a casual, freewheeling, relaxed get-together of friends. I would set the table with whatever felt comfortable but I would certainly have a large bouquet of flowers, picked from your own backyard if possible.

For music you might want to put together a string of California songs including "California Dreaming," "If You're Going to San Francisco," "Do You Know the Way to San Jose?," or maybe just put on the Beach Boys and leave it at that.

British Isles Sunday Brunch

Breakfast better than the Queen herself gets.

SERVES 4

☐ Champagne and Freshly Squeezed Orange Juice
☐ Scrambled Eggs with Herbs and Tomato
☐ Mixed Breakfast Grill
☐ Irish Soda Bread
☐ Sweet Country Butter and a Variety of Jams and Preserves
☐ Irish or English Breakfast Tea

CHAMPAGNE AND FRESHLY SQUEEZED ORANGE JUICE

4 to 6 juice oranges

2 bottles good-quality French, California, or Spanish champagne

1. Squeeze the juice from the oranges, removing the pits but saving as much pulp as possible. Place 1 ounce juice in each tall fluted champagne glass. Fill the glasses with champagne and serve.

SCRAMBLED EGGS
WITH HERBS AND TOMATO

8 large farm-fresh eggs, bought at
   your local farmers' market if
   possible
1 teaspoon Dijon mustard
1 tablespoon minced fresh parsley
1 teaspoon minced fresh chives or
   dill (do not use dried herbs in
   this dish)

Salt and pepper to taste
2 medium-sized fresh tomatoes
1 teaspoon olive oil

1. Crack the eggs into a medium mixing bowl. Beat to combine the yolks and whites. Add 3 tablespoons cold water, mustard, herbs, salt, and pepper. Beat thoroughly.

2. Cut the cores from the tomatoes. Cut the tomatoes in half and remove the seeds and juice and discard. Finely chop the remaining tomato.

3. Place the skillet over medium heat for 2 to 3 minutes until it is hot but not smoking. Add the olive oil to the pan and swirl it around with the spatula. Add the eggs and scramble them. When the eggs are half done but still very runny, add the chopped tomato and cook until done.

MIXED BREAKFAST GRILL

8 slices thick country bacon

6 to 8 sausages, preferably a
   mixture of English bangers,
   bratwurst, chorizo, small
   kielbasa, and venison or duck
   sausages

1. Preheat the broiler. Place the bacon and sausages on the broiler pan and broil 4 to 6 inches from the heat source. You may need to do this in 2 batches. Remove to a skillet, cover, and keep warm.

IRISH SODA BREAD

4 cups unbleached flour
2½ teaspoons salt
1 teaspoon baking soda
⅓ cup sugar
1 cup currants or raisins

1 tablespoon caraway seeds
(optional)
2 cups buttermilk
1 egg

1. Preheat the oven to 350°F. In a large mixing bowl, combine the flour, salt, baking soda, sugar, currants, and caraway seeds. Stir to blend well.

2. In a small mixing bowl, combine the buttermilk and egg. Beat and stir to blend well.

3. Pour the liquid into the flour mixture and stir, scraping the sides to form a ball of dough. Turn the dough out onto a flat floured surface and knead for 5 to 10 minutes. You will need to add extra flour to prevent sticking.

4. Form the dough into a round loaf and place it on a buttered baking sheet. Put it in the oven and bake for 35 to 40 minutes. Cool and slice.

PULLING IT ALL TOGETHER

This is a very simple bacon and eggs brunch that is elevated by carefully choosing the finest ingredients. Even including the bread, this meal will take only an hour's time to prepare.

Before you get involved in making the bread, squeeze the oranges. Place the juice in a container, cover, and put in the refrigerator.

Make the Irish soda bread. While it is baking you can set the table and place the jams and preserves in their serving bowls.

With luck, your guests will arrive just as the bread comes out of the oven, and fills the house with that wonderful aroma. Give your guests a mimosa. After you have removed the bread, turn the oven to broil and cook the bacon and sausages.

While the meats are broiling, chop the tomatoes, prepare the herbs, and stir the eggs in the bowl. Get the skillet out and let it begin to warm up on top of the stove.

Start making the tea. Put the kettle of water on to boil. When the water is quite hot, pour about $1/3$ cup into the teapot, swirl it around, and dump it out. This warms the pot. Now, add 3 teaspoons of loose tea, 1 for me, 1 for thee, and 1 for the pot. Pour the boiling water into the pot and replace the lid. Let the tea steep for 5 minutes, and pour carefully. Serve with whole milk and sugar cubes, 1 or 2 lumps.

Start the eggs when the sausages are done and draining on paper towels. Scramble the eggs and serve them and the sausages on one large platter. Let people help themselves to what they want.

Slice the soda bread and serve on a plate along with the butter.

BEVERAGES. When you are buying the oranges for the mimosas, look to see if there are any blood oranges or tangelos that you could use to add a different flavor to the drink.

The better the quality of champagne you use, the better the drink, up to a point. I wouldn't spend more than $10 for each bottle. Probably the Spanish champagnes in that category are your best buy.

AMBIENCE. The ideal Sunday brunch spot is a light and airy sunroom that overlooks a springtime garden. Small vases of tiny flowers should grace a charming table.

Restaurants play soft quiet music at Sunday brunches for a reason. It helps soothe people's way into the day. Play some baroque or Renaissance music featuring the harpsichord or the recorder. Let your guests help you set the table and serve the food.

Make a special effort to find a variety of British or Irish jams and preserves. You must have a jar of tart Seville orange marmalade. Good labels are Frank Cooper's Oxford Coarse Cut, Dundee, Chivers, and Elsenham. Other British jam favorites include gooseberry, blackberry, and currant.

Now that you have spent a fortune on jams, display them by spooning them into individual jam pots or small crystal bowls.

■ Autumn Weekend Tailgate ■

An autumn tailgate meal has to be as easy and portable as any summer picnic while being hearty enough to satisfy brisk-weather appetites.

SERVES 6

☐ Creamy Carrot Soup
☐ Roast Beef Tenderloin
☐ Dilled Potato Salad with Salmon Caviar
☐ Savoy Cabbage Cole Slaw
☐ Chocolate Brownies

■ CREAMY CARROT SOUP ■

6 strips thick-cut smoked bacon
1 pound carrots, peeled and
    coarsely chopped
1 cup coarsely chopped celery
1 medium onion, peeled and
    chopped
1 clove garlic, peeled and minced

2 cups chopped fresh mushrooms
1 bay leaf
½ teaspoon dried thyme
2 quarts chicken stock, canned or
    homemade
Salt and pepper to taste
1 pint half-and-half

1. Chop the bacon into ⅓-inch strips. Place the strips in the bottom of a large soup pot and fry over medium heat until crisp. Remove the bacon from the pot and pour off all but 2 tablespoons of the drippings.

2. Add the carrots, celery, onion, garlic, and mushrooms to the pot. Fry over medium heat for 5 to 8 minutes until the onions are soft and translucent.

3. Add the bay leaf, thyme, and chicken stock. Bring to the boil, turn down to medium-low, and simmer the soup for 15 minutes. Turn off the heat and let cool to room temperature.

4. Purée the soup in a food processor in small batches and return to the pot. Add the bacon, salt, and pepper. Add the half-and-half and heat the soup to almost boiling. Do not boil or the half-and-half will curdle.

81

ROAST BEEF TENDERLOIN

1 whole tenderloin of beef,
    approximately 4 to 5 pounds
2 tablespoons olive oil

1 clove garlic, peeled and minced
Salt and freshly ground black
    pepper to taste

1. Preheat the oven to 375°F. Rub the tenderloin all over with the oil, garlic, salt, and pepper. Place the meat in a low-sided roasting pan, put it in the oven, and roast for 25 to 30 minutes, or until the meat thermometer reads 125°F. to 130°F.

2. Remove the meat from the oven, cover with foil, and let rest for 15 minutes.

DILLED POTATO SALAD
WITH SALMON CAVIAR

12 medium-sized red waxy
    potatoes
1/2 cup mayonnaise
3/4 cup plain yogurt or sour cream
1 medium-sized red onion, peeled
    and chopped fine

2 tablespoons minced fresh dill or
    1 teaspoon dried dill weed
2 ounces red salmon caviar
Salt and freshly ground black
    pepper to taste

1. Place the potatoes in a large pot with water to cover and boil until tender, about 20 minutes. Drain and cool.

2. Peel the potatoes, if you like, and cut them into 1/2-inch cubes. Place them in a medium mixing bowl.

3. Blend the remaining ingredients in a separate bowl. Be careful not to break the salmon caviar.

4. Combine the dressing with the potatoes, folding carefully.

SAVOY CABBAGE COLE SLAW

1 large head Savoy cabbage
1 medium red onion, peeled and
    finely chopped
2 large red or green bell peppers,
    cored, seeded, and finely
    chopped
3/4 cup granulated sugar

1 tablespoon salt
1 teaspoon dry mustard
2 teaspoons celery seeds
1 cup white wine vinegar
1/2 cup olive oil
Freshly ground black pepper

1. Cut the cabbage into quarters and remove the inner core. Shred the cabbage. Mix the cabbage with the onion and peppers in a large mixing bowl.

2. In a noncorrosive saucepan, mix the sugar, salt, mustard, celery seeds, vinegar, oil, and pepper. Bring the mixture to the boil and stir to dissolve the sugar.

3. Pour the sauce over the cabbage and mix well.

CHOCOLATE BROWNIES

Four 1-ounce squares unsweetened
    chocolate
1 1/2 sticks (3/4 cup) unsalted butter
4 eggs
2 cups granulated sugar

1/4 teaspoon salt
1 teaspoon vanilla extract
1 cup sifted all-purpose flour
1 cup walnut or pecan pieces

1. Preheat the oven to 350°F. Rub butter all over the inside of a 9-inch-square baking pan. Sprinkle a tablespoon of flour in the pan and shake that around to dust the pan.

2. Melt the chocolate and butter in a double boiler or saucepan over very low heat. Watch carefully and stir to blend well.

3. In a mixing bowl, beat the eggs until light and fluffy. Add the sugar, salt, and vanilla. Beat again until light and fluffy.

4. Stir in the chocolate mixture, then the flour, stirring well after each addition. Fold in the nuts.

5. Pour the batter into the pan and bake for 30 minutes. Remove, cool, and cut into squares.

PULLING IT ALL TOGETHER

The important thing to remember with this meal is that it has to be packed and taken along to your autumn weekend destination, probably a football game or other sporting event, a parents' or alumni weekend at college, antiquing, or just a weekend of "leaf peeping" at the colorful trees in the countryside.

Things have to be kept warm or cold and be just as delicious when you serve them as when you cooked them. You are going to need a large thermos-type container for the soup because that needs to be kept hot. The rest of the food needs to be kept cold in a cooler.

Back in the kitchen, make the creamy carrot soup first, up to the point where you add the half-and-half. Cover and let rest. Add the half-and-half and reheat the soup just before pouring it into the thermos.

Next make the potato salad and the cole slaw. Put each in its respective hard plastic container and place in the refrigerator.

Make the brownies and let them cool completely before you wrap them in waxed paper first and then in aluminum foil. They can also be made the day before.

Roast the tenderloin, let it cool, and then carve it into $1/2$- to $3/4$-inch-thick slices. Reshape the tenderloin and double-wrap it in aluminum foil.

BEVERAGES. Because you are going to be driving, you should not drink any alcoholic beverages with your meal and then drive. The way to get around this is to appoint a designated driver who will drink no alcohol so that the rest of you can.

Serve unflavored bottled water, both bubbly and still, for the designated driver and for those who want no alcohol. Back this up with a thermos of hot coffee.

Bring along a couple of bottles of robust red wine to serve for those who do want wine. A Spanish Rioja, an Australian Shiraz, or a California Cabernet Sauvignon would stand up to the beef and the brisk autumn weather.

If it is a particularly chilly day, include a small bottle of Calvados or French Cognac or Armagnac.

AMBIENCE. A weekend tailgate party does not mean you have to stand in a parking lot and eat with your fingers. A folding table and some folding stools can fit in the car's trunk. So can a couple of large woolen blankets that can be spread under one of those colorful maple trees.

If you want to use hard plates, try something colorful like Fiesta Ware. There are plenty of very firm plastic and paper plates, and many of them are quite good-looking. Don't forget plastic cutlery.

Be sure to bring heat-resistant plastic or paper cups to serve the soup in.

Then, just get to where you are going, set out the food, and let everyone dig in.

■ The Big Easy ■

After eating this, you'll feel like dancing at a Cajun fais-dodo.

SERVES 4

- ☐ Shrimp Rémoulade
- ☐ Louisiana Crab Cakes with Creole Sauce
- ☐ Zucchini-Squash Sauté
- ☐ Pecan Pie with Vanilla Ice Cream

SHRIMP RÉMOULADE

24 medium shrimp, about ¾
    pound, shells on
4 large lettuce leaves
2 egg yolks
Juice of ½ lemon
½ cup olive oil
½ cup minced celery
½ cup minced fresh parsley

½ cup minced scallions
½ cup vegetable oil (safflower,
    sunflower, or other)
2 tablespoons Creole or other
    brown mustard
2 tablespoons prepared horseradish
1 teaspoon paprika
1 tablespoon white wine vinegar

1. Bring 1 quart of water to a boil in a large pot. Add the shrimp, turn off the heat, cover, and let rest 10 minutes. Drain, cool, and peel.

2. Wash, drain, and dry the lettuce leaves. Wrap in paper towels and refrigerate.

3. Place the egg yolks and lemon juice in a blender or food processor. Blend at slow speed for 30 seconds. With the motor running, add the olive oil a tablespoon at a time. Turn off the motor.

4. Add the celery, parsley, and scallions and blend at medium speed for 1 minute, or until the vegetables are puréed into the sauce. With the motor running at slow speed, add the vegetable oil a tablespoon at a time. Turn off the motor and spoon the sauce into a mixing bowl.

5. Add the remaining ingredients and stir carefully. Taste and adjust seasoning.

6. Mix the shrimp with the rémoulade sauce, tossing to coat well. Place a lettuce leaf on each of 4 salad plates to form a cup. Scoop out equal portions of shrimp rémoulade onto each lettuce leaf and serve.

CRAB CAKES WITH CREOLE SAUCE

1 pound lump or backfin crabmeat
2 eggs, beaten
1 cup fresh, unseasoned bread crumbs (make your own if possible)
1/4 teaspoon each paprika, dried thyme, salt, and black pepper

1 teaspoon each Worcestershire sauce and Creole or other brown mustard
1 tablespoon mayonnaise
2 tablespoons vegetable oil

1. Place the crabmeat in a medium mixing bowl. Pick through carefully to remove any small bits of cartilage or shell.

2. Add the remaining ingredients except the oil to the crabmeat and stir well to combine. Form the mixture into 8 patties. Place on a sheet of wax paper.

3. Place a large skillet over medium-high heat for 2 minutes. Add the vegetable oil and heat for 1 minute. Add the crab cakes and fry until nicely brown, about 1 minute on each side. Don't overcook or they will dry out. Remove to plates and serve with Creole Sauce on the side or underneath.

CREOLE SAUCE

3 tablespoons olive or vegetable oil
¾ cup each finely chopped onion,
    celery, and green bell pepper
3 cloves garlic, peeled and minced
½ teaspoon each dried thyme,
    cayenne pepper, salt, and black
    pepper

One 28-ounce can Italian plum
    tomatoes
1 cup fresh or frozen corn kernels
    (optional)

1. Heat the olive oil in a 2-quart saucepan over medium-high heat for 2 minutes. Add the onion, celery, and bell pepper and sauté for 5 minutes, stirring often.

2. Add the garlic and sauté 1 minute. Add the thyme, cayenne, salt, black pepper, and the canned tomatoes. Bring the sauce to the boil, lower the heat to medium, and simmer for 15 minutes. Stir often and crush the tomatoes when you do.

3. Add the corn and simmer for 5 minutes. Serve underneath or next to the crab cakes.

ZUCCHINI-SQUASH SAUTÉ

3 cups mixed zucchini and yellow
    summer squash, sliced into
    half-moons

2 tablespoons olive oil
Salt and pepper to taste

1. Heat the olive oil in a large skillet over medium-high heat for 3 minutes. Add the squash and stir-fry for 3 to 5 minutes, or until the squash is tender but still firm.

2. Sprinkle on the salt and pepper, stir, and serve.

PECAN PIE

1 unbaked 9-inch pie shell
3 eggs
3/4 cup granulated sugar
1/4 teaspoon salt

1/3 cup melted butter
1 cup dark corn syrup
1 teaspoon vanilla extract
1 cup pecan halves

1. Preheat the oven to 450°F.

2. Place the eggs, sugar, salt, melted butter, corn syrup, and vanilla extract in a mixing bowl and beat thoroughly. Add the pecans and stir to blend well.

3. Pour the ingredients into the pie shell and place in the oven. Reduce the heat to 375°F. and bake 40 to 50 minutes or until a knife comes out clean when inserted into the center of the pie. Cool and serve with vanilla ice cream.

You can make this meal a little bit easier on yourself by buying the pecan pie. I suggest you buy the ice cream. And you can certainly buy a premade crust for the pie if you like. Then the meal is really easy; except for the pecan pie, it can all be cooked in less than an hour. Make the pie early in the day and set it aside at room temperature.

The secret to success with this meal is not overcooking the shrimp and crab cakes, which would make them tough and dry.

Make the Creole Sauce first, giving the flavors a chance to mingle and develop.

Then cook the shrimp. While they are cooling, make the rémoulade sauce. Peeling the shrimp will take about 10 minutes, but once you get the hang of it the work goes pretty fast. Toss the shrimp with the sauce. Wash the lettuce leaves.

I feel very strongly that you should make the crab cakes at the very last minute because they tend to dry out if you make them ahead of time. With that in mind, cook the zucchini and squash until they are almost done, cover, and keep warm.

Measure and prepare all the ingredients for the crab cakes. After you and your guests have enjoyed the shrimp rémoulade, then you can make the crab cakes. When the last crab cake is in the skillet, reheat the zucchini and squash. Serve the crab cakes, Creole Sauce, and squash on the same individual plates and bring them all to the table.

Clear the table and serve the pecan pie, ice cream, and coffee.

BEVERAGES. New Orleans has its own peculiar mixed drinks, the Hurricane, the Ramos Gin Fizz, and the Sazerac. I think the only one worth drinking at this dinner party is the Sazerac, which is based on bourbon or sometimes rye whiskey. Many New Yorkers call Canadian whiskey rye whiskey. It is not. Get real rye whiskey, like Old Overhold or Jim Beam rye.

Sazerac: For each serving, use 1½ ounces bourbon or rye whiskey, 2 drops Angostura bitters, 2 drops Peychaud bitters, ¼ teaspoon confectioners' sugar, 1 teaspoon Pernod, and a twist of lemon or orange peel. Fill a cocktail shaker with all the ingredients except the twist. Stir to blend well. Fill a short heavy glass with ice. Pour the drink over the ice and garnish with the twist.

I would not serve a challenging or expensive bottle of wine with this meal. I would serve a nicely chilled white wine, probably a French Muscadet, Vouvray, or Sancerre, or a California Sauvignon Blanc.

Chilled Beaujolais would be a good red wine.

You must serve New Orleans chicory coffee with dessert. French Market and Luzianne are widely available brands. Chicory coffee is rich, thick, and black. You will want to serve it with hot milk and sugar, as café au lait, as they do at the French Market in New Orleans.

AMBIENCE. New Orleans is a lively city that is known as the deepest point of the American South and the northern point of the Caribbean. Some of the restaurants there are gaudy, some are refined in a European tradition, and some are funky roadhouses. I think you should take the high road and go for a look that is refined, like Galatoire's, Antoine's, or Arnaud's. You're trying for an old-fashioned French restaurant with a Southern accent.

Dress the table with a heavy white cotton cloth and use napkins to match. Flickering gas lamps are a part of old New Orleans. Think about getting a clean, new, pretty kerosene lamp instead of candles for the tables. (Be sure to get fuel that does not smell.)

Music is easy. The soundtrack for the film *The Big Easy* is a nice collection of New Orleans songs. Other good New Orleans musicians are Fats Domino, Professor Long Hair, Buckwheat Zydeco, Clifton Chenier, Louis Armstrong, Jelly Roll Morton, Pete Fountain, Al Hirt, and the Preservation Hall Jazz Band.

Tex-Mex Brunch ■

This is what folks in Austin would like to eat on a Sunday morning.

SERVES 4

- ☐ Gulf of Mexico Seafood Cocktail
- ☐ Huevos Rancheros
- ☐ Brownsville Fried Potatoes
- ☐ Rio Grande Citrus Salad
- ☐ Café con Chocolate

GULF OF MEXICO SEAFOOD COCKTAIL

1 pound small to medium shrimp,
  shells on, or fresh crabmeat, or
  24 small oysters or clams, or a
  combination
1 cup bottled chili sauce
1 jalapeño pepper, seeded and
  minced
1 medium-sized ripe tomato, cored
  and chopped fine

1 tablespoon minced fresh parsley
1 tablespoon minced fresh cilantro
Juice of 1 lime
2 drops Tabasco sauce
½ teaspoon freshly ground black
  pepper
Lime or lemon wedges for garnish

1. Bring 2 quarts of water to the boil in a large pot and add the shrimp with their shells on. Turn off the heat, cover, and let rest for 10 minutes. Drain, let cool, and peel the shrimp.

2. Buy clams and oysters that have been previously shucked or have the fishmonger do it for you. Pick over the crab to remove any shell.

3. Make the sauce by combining the chili sauce with the jalapeño pepper, tomato, parsley, cilantro, lime juice, Tabasco sauce, and black pepper. Stir and let rest 5 minutes.

4. Add the peeled shrimp, crabmeat, oysters, clams, or a combination to

93

the sauce. Stir well. Spoon the mixture into wide-mouth champagne or wine glasses and garnish with a lime or lemon wedge.

HUEVOS RANCHEROS

1 small red onion, peeled and
    chopped fine
3 cloves garlic, peeled and minced
2 jalapeño peppers, seeded and
    chopped fine
1 small green or red bell pepper,
    cored, seeded, and chopped
    fine
3 tablespoons olive, corn, or other
    vegetable oil
2 tablespoons each minced fresh
    parsley and fresh cilantro
1/4 to 1/2 pound chorizo sausage or
    other smoked pork sausage,
    chopped

1 teaspoon chili powder
4 medium-sized ripe tomatoes or
    one 28-ounce can whole
    tomatoes, drained
1/2 teaspoon each salt and pepper
8 best-quality fresh corn tortillas
    from the refrigerator case at
    the supermarket (fried and
    dried taco tortillas will not
    work)
8 ounces Monterey Jack,
    Manchego, queso blanco, or
    white or yellow Cheddar
    cheese
8 eggs

1. Make the ranchero sauce by frying the onion, garlic, and peppers in the oil in a large skillet over medium-high heat for 5 minutes. Add the parsley, cilantro, and sausage and fry for another 5 minutes. Add the chili powder, tomatoes, salt, and pepper. Fry for another 5 minutes, stirring and mashing the tomatoes to make a thick sauce.

2. Wrap the tortillas in foil and warm them in the oven at 350°F. for 10 minutes.

3. Slice or grate the cheese and fry the eggs sunny side up.

4. To assemble, place a tortilla on a metal plate or pie pan that can be slipped under the broiler. Cover with a spoonful of sauce. Top with 2 eggs, cover with another tortilla. Scoop 2 or 3 spoonfuls of sauce on the top tortilla, cover with cheese, and broil 6 inches from the heat element until the cheese melts and browns. Repeat for each serving with all the remaining ingredients, and serve.

BROWNSVILLE FRIED POTATOES

6 medium-sized white potatoes
3 tablespoons olive, corn, or other
   vegetable oil
1/2 medium-sized red onion, peeled
   and chopped fine

1/2 green or red bell pepper, seeded
   and chopped fine
Salt and pepper to taste

1. Wash the potatoes and peel them if you like. Place them in a large pot, cover with water, and boil them for 10 to 15 minutes or until they are tender but still firm. Drain and cool. It is best to do this the night before.

2. Dice the potatoes into 1/2-inch chunks or coarsely chop them. Warm the oil over medium-high heat in a large heavy skillet for 2 minutes. Add the potatoes and fry, turning only once or twice, for 10 minutes or until golden brown. Crowding the potatoes in too small a skillet will cause them to get gummy, not brown.

3. Add the onion, bell pepper, salt, and pepper. Fry for 3 minutes, stirring occasionally.

RIO GRANDE CITRUS SALAD

1 large white grapefruit
1 large pink grapefruit
2 tangerines

1 Temple or other orange
1/2 teaspoon sugar
1/8 teaspoon ground cinnamon

1. Peel the fruit and pare off any rind or white membranes. Pull into sections. Cut the sections into bite-sized pieces and place in a large fruit bowl.

2. Sprinkle with the sugar and cinnamon, stir, and let rest for 30 minutes for the juices to mingle.

CAFÉ CON CHOCOLATE

1 quart regular American coffee
3 ounces Mexican chocolate or
  semisweet baker's chocolate

$1/4$ teaspoon ground cinnamon
2 cups whole milk

1. Make the American coffee and keep warm. Melt the chocolate in a 3- to 4-quart saucepan with 1 tablespoon of water and the cinnamon. Add the milk and heat through. Add the coffee and heat to near boiling. Stir and serve.

Boil the potatoes the night before or as early as possible on the day of the brunch. Long before your guests arrive make the citrus salad, the café con chocolate, and the sauce for the huevos rancheros. You can make the seafood sauce before your guests arrive but don't add the seafood to the sauce until they come.

Make the potatoes, cover, and keep warm.

When your guests do arrive, serve them tequila sunrises or mango bellinis. Call your guests to the table, mix the seafood with the sauce, and serve the seafood cocktails.

Fry the eggs and assemble the huevos rancheros.

Reheat the potatoes and place the huevos under the broiler. Serve the huevos on individual plates but pass the potatoes in a bowl.

Start serving the café con chocolate along with the huevos. Clear the table and serve the citrus salad.

BEVERAGES. Tequila Sunrise: Fill a tall highball glass with cracked ice. Add 1 ounce tequila and fill the glass with orange juice. Stir well. Top with ½ ounce grenadine. Garnish with a cherry or slice of lime.

Mango Bellini: Pour 1 ounce mango juice into a tall flute glass. Fill with chilled champagne or sparkling wine and serve.

AMBIENCE. Think of yourself as a guest in a slightly faded grand old hotel in a town along the Mexico–United States border. You're in the cool shade of a courtyard full of light. Set the table with a nice white tablecloth and blue-and-white-checked napkins. Try to find rustic pottery plates and cups.

A beautiful flower arrangement with large exotic flowers like bird of paradise or gladiolus should be nearby. Encourage your guests to wear white linen and dark glasses. Play norteño music with accordion and trumpets in the background.

■ Southwestern Dinner ■

*This Southwest may exist only in the minds of the young chefs
who created the cuisine, but who cares!*

SERVES 4

☐ Chili Corn Chowder with Chorizo
☐ Broiled Catfish with Black Bean Tomatillo Relish
☐ Green and Yellow Squash Sauté
☐ Blue Corn Sticks
☐ Watermelon Ice

CHILI CORN CHOWDER WITH CHORIZO

1 tablespoon olive, corn, or other
   vegetable oil
2 chorizo sausages, sliced thin
1 medium-sized red onion, peeled
   and chopped small
2 jalapeño or serrano peppers,
   seeded and sliced thin
1 large green or red bell pepper,
   cored, seeded, and chopped
   fine

3 cups corn kernels cut from about
   6 ears
½ teaspoon each salt and black
   pepper
2 tablespoons all-purpose flour
3 cups milk

1. Heat the oil in 4-quart soup pot and add the chorizo, onion, and peppers. Sauté over medium heat 5 minutes, stirring often.

2. Add the corn, salt, pepper, and flour, stirring well to incorporate the flour into the vegetables. Cook 2 minutes and add the milk. Stir and cook over medium heat 10 minutes. Cover and keep warm.

BROILED CATFISH WITH
BLACK BEAN TOMATILLO RELISH

FOR THE RELISH:

1 cup tomatillos, husks removed, finely chopped

1/2 cup canned black beans, drained and rinsed

1/2 cup chopped fresh tomato

1/2 cup chopped red or green bell pepper

1 small seedless orange, peeled and chopped fine

Juice of 1 lemon

2 tablespoons each finely chopped fresh parsley and cilantro

1/4 teaspoon each salt and pepper

3 tablespoons olive oil

2 tablespoons vegetable oil

4 catfish fillets, 6 to 8 ounces each

Salt and pepper to taste

1 teaspoon paprika or mild chili powder

1. Combine all the ingredients for the relish in a mixing bowl and set aside. Cover and let rest for 20 to 30 minutes.

2. Preheat the broiler. Spread the oil on the fish and sprinkle with the salt, pepper, and chili powder. Broil the fillets 6 inches from the heat source for 4 minutes, turn and broil for another 3 minutes.

3. Serve 1 fillet on each plate and spoon the relish on the side or on top.

GREEN AND YELLOW SQUASH SAUTÉ

One 6-inch-long green zucchini squash

One 6-inch-long yellow summer squash

2 tablespoons butter

Salt and pepper to taste

1. The quality and type of squash you use makes the difference in this dish. If you can find finger-sized baby green or yellow squash, by all means use them but remember to buy 6 little ones to replace 1 big one.

2. Wash and dry the squash. Slice into bite-sized chunks or half moons,

or leave whole if using baby squash. Melt the butter in a large skillet, add the squash, and sauté over medium-high heat for 3 to 5 minutes. Add the salt and pepper and serve.

BLUE CORN STICKS

■━━■

You need the heavy cast-iron corn-stick bakeware to make corn sticks. Otherwise, use a cast-iron skillet or a 9-inch baking pan to make one large corn cake, and lengthen the time in the oven.

1 cup blue cornmeal
1 cup all-purpose wheat flour
1 tablespoon sugar
1 teaspoon salt
1 tablespoon baking powder

2 eggs
1 cup milk or buttermilk
¼ cup vegetable oil or melted
  butter

1. Preheat oven to 425°F. Brush the pans liberally with corn oil. Place corn-stick pans in the oven while you make the batter.

2. In a large bowl, mix together the cornmeal, flour, sugar, salt, and baking powder. In a separate bowl, beat the eggs lightly and add the milk or buttermilk and oil or butter. Pour the wet mixture into the dry and beat until smooth. Don't overmix.

3. Pull the hot corn-stick pans out of the oven. Fill with the batter. Return to the oven and bake 15 to 20 minutes or until golden brown. Remove from pans and cool. Makes 14.

WATERMELON ICE

3 cups fresh watermelon, seeded
   and chopped
Juice of ½ lemon

2 tablespoons sugar
Watermelon slices and mint sprigs
   for garnish (optional)

1. Place the watermelon, lemon juice, and sugar in a blender or food processor. Whir to form a smooth, creamy slush.

2. Place the slush in a stainless-steel bowl and put in freezer. After 30 minutes, remove the slush, beat it, and return to freezer. Do this three times and you are ready to serve.

3. Spoon the watermelon ice into stemmed wineglasses and garnish with a slice of fresh watermelon and a sprig of mint.

Make the watermelon ice first because it takes from 1½ to 2 hours of freezing time. The soup and the blue corn sticks can be made a day ahead of time, covered and wrapped, and refrigerated. Otherwise make the black bean relish, then make the soup, and then make the corn sticks. Chop the squash.

When your guests have arrived, serve them a beverage and head for the kitchen. Reheat the soup and the corn sticks.

Make the broiled catfish and sauté the squash at the same time. Take the catfish out of the broiler, cover with foil, and keep warm.

Serve the soup, then serve the catfish, relish, and squash on plates and serve the corn sticks in the corn-stick baking pans.

Clear the table and serve the watermelon ice.

BEVERAGES. Southwestern drinking habits are quite similar to Mexican but with a stronger American overtone. I would suggest a not too oaky California Chardonnay, a California Sauvignon Blanc, or a white zinfandel. One of the new American amber-style beers would be good; try Samuel Adams, Sierra Nevada, Anchor Steam, or the Mexican beer Dos Equis.

AMBIENCE. The Southwestern culinary region seems to extend from Dallas to Santa Fe and into Arizona, plus anywhere chefs get the inspiration. A long woven garland of dried chili peppers called a ristra is a must for decor, plus cactus plants and aloe vera. Think Georgia O'Keeffe and her pastel desert pinks, blues, and beiges. Colorful Navajo weavings and turquoise come to mind.

You might try some desert Indian ceremonial music to set a unique tone at first, but then shift into Texas two-step and waltz music with fiddles and guitars and probably an accordion.

Beaujolais Nouveau Est Arrivé

A dinner party to celebrate the arrival of the first Beaujolais nouveau wine from France, to be held in the middle of November when the bottles are released and ready to be consumed.

SERVES 4

☐ Coquilles St.-Jacques—Tiny scallops in cream sauce
☐ Pan-Grilled Steak
☐ Frites—Slender french fries
☐ Mesclun Salad Vinaigrette
☐ Roquefort Cheese and Fresh Ripe Pears

COQUILLES ST.-JACQUES

2 cups dry white wine
1 pound small bay or calico
   scallops
2 shallots, peeled and minced
2 tablespoons butter

1 tablespoon flour
2 tablespoons dry sherry
Salt and pepper to taste
2 tablespoons grated Parmesan
   cheese

1. Bring the wine to a boil in a medium-sized saucepan. Add the scallops, return to the boil, cover, and turn off the heat. Let scallops sit in the hot wine for 5 minutes and remove, reserving the wine.

2. In a separate saucepan, sauté the shallots with the butter over medium heat 2 minutes. Add the flour and stir to form a paste, or roux. Cook this for 2 minutes, stirring often. Add the sherry and 1 cup of the reserved wine and stir to form a smooth, creamy sauce. You may have to add a little more wine. Add salt and pepper.

3. Butter four large scallop shells or ramekins. Fill each with scallops. Spoon the sauce over the scallops and sprinkle with Parmesan cheese. Place

103

the scallop shells 6 inches under the broiler and broil for 3 to 5 minutes, or until the cheese melts and browns a little. Serve.

PAN-GRILLED STEAK

1 top-quality boneless sirloin
    steak, 1½ inches thick (about
    2 pounds), or four ½-pound rib
    eye or club steaks
2 tablespoons olive oil
½ teaspoon salt

1 teaspoon freshly ground black
    pepper
1 tablespoon minced fresh shallots
½ cup Beaujolais nouveau
2 tablespoons Cognac
2 tablespoons unsalted butter

1. Rub both sides of the steak with olive oil, salt, and pepper. Place a large heavy skillet over high heat and heat it until smoking, usually about 3 to 5 minutes.

2. Place the steak in the skillet, keep the heat on high, and cook 5 minutes. Turn the steak over and continue cooking an additional 4 minutes, for medium-rare, as this steak should be. Remove the steak from the skillet and keep warm.

3. Lower the heat to medium and sauté the shallots in the pan drippings for 2 minutes. Add the Beaujolais and boil about 3 minutes, until the wine gets thick and syrupy.

4. Add the Cognac to the skillet and ignite. When the flames die down add the butter and stir, thickening the sauce. Pour the sauce over the steak, slice into serving pieces, and serve.

FRITES

4 or 5 medium-sized white potatoes

One 24-ounce bottle vegetable oil (safflower, canola, peanut, sunflower, or a blend are good choices)

1. Wash and peel the potatoes. Cut them into long, thin strips, put them in a bowl of lukewarm water, and soak them for 30 minutes. Drain and dry thoroughly.

2. Heat the oil in a large deep pot or wok to 375°F. or until it starts to smoke slightly and a potato strip pops and sizzles when tossed in. Cook the potatoes in two batches without overcrowding them. Stir the frites around often with a slotted spoon. This helps them to brown evenly. Drain the frites well on paper towels.

3. Reheat the oil to 375°F. Return all the frites to the hot oil and cook quickly to make them crisp. Drain again and serve.

MESCLUN SALAD VINAIGRETTE

4 cups mixed salad greens, such as mâche, rocket, mizuna, curly endive, basil leaves, red leaf lettuce, young dandelion greens, watercress, nasturtium leaves, chives, immature chicory, and Boston lettuce (some stores have ready-made mesclun blends)

6 tablespoons light French olive oil
2 tablespoons red wine vinegar
Salt and pepper to taste

1. Wash and drain all the salad greens. Dry on paper towels.

2. Pour the olive oil, vinegar, salt, and pepper into a large wooden salad bowl. Whisk the ingredients to make a smooth creamy dressing. Cross the

salad forks over the dressing and place the greens over the forks, keeping it away from the dressing if possible.

3. Bring the salad to the table and toss it at the last moment. Serve.

ROQUEFORT CHEESE
AND FRESH RIPE PEARS

Because it is made with sheep's milk, Roquefort has a very special tang that perfectly complements ripe pears. But it is expensive, so use whatever bleu cheese, foreign or domestic, that you prefer.

¼ pound Roquefort cheese
4 ripe pears
Rolls of crusty French bread

½ stick (4 tablespoons) unsalted
butter

1. Give each person a wedge of Roquefort, a pear, a roll, and a tablespoon of unsalted butter. Some French people like to mix their bleu cheese with butter to make a creamy spread for the bread or the pear.

The most challenging part of your party will be obtaining the wine on the very day it becomes available in your city. The remedy is to place an advance order with your wine merchant. Remember to chill the wine for at least 3 to 4 hours so it will be cold when you serve it.

Buy the pears 2 or 3 days beforehand and let them ripen at room temperature.

Make the Coquilles St.-Jacques up to the point where they are to go under the broiler. Cover and leave at room temperature. Slice the potatoes and put them in to soak. Make the salad but do not toss.

You have to make the frites and the steak at the same time, so have all the ingredients for the steak premeasured and ready to hand. Pan-grill the steak but don't make the sauce. Fry the frites and drain them but don't put them in for their last quick browning. Cover and keep warm.

Call your guests to the table and make a big deal out of opening the first bottles of Beaujolais nouveau. Return to the kitchen and brown the scallops under the broiler and serve.

Make another toast to the Beaujolais wine and return to the kitchen to finish the steak sauce and the second browning of the frites. Serve.

Clear the table and serve the salad. Clear the table and serve the cheese and fruit.

BEVERAGES. Beaujolais is a region in east-central France situated between the Burgundy and Côtes-du-Rhône wine-growing regions. It is famous for great steaks and fruity red wine. The wine is light, fresh-tasting, with a flowery bouquet with hints of peaches and roses. It has a very purple color.

Beaujolais nouveau, also known as primeur, is the first wine that is drunk just 4 to 6 weeks after the grape harvest. November 15 is the official date set by the French government when the wine can be released to the public. Until the 1960s, when Beaujolais nouveau became popular in France, it was sold by the glass from barrels in the region where it was grown. Now it is bottled and shipped all over the world.

The more mature Beaujolais, not sold as nouveau, is labeled as Beaujolais-Villages, or more specifically under the town names of Saint-Amour, Julienas,

Chénas, Moulin-à-Vent, Fleurie, Chiroubles, Morgon, Brouilly, and Côte de Brouilly.

AMBIENCE. Think of the charming, rustic atmosphere of a French country inn. Beaujolais nouveau is not a wine to be revered. It is meant to be unpretentiously sloshed down with an air of celebration.

Think of a blue-checkered tablecloth with dried flowers in a wicker basket. Candles are all right as long as they are not too imposing. Serve the steak-frites on oval steak plates along with steak knives. Serve the wine in wide tulip-shaped stemmed glasses or in short clear juice glasses.

A Beaujolais nouveau party does not demand any special type of music. Play what you like or just let the sound of friends' laughter and conversation fill the room.

Antipasto Buffet ∎

With antipasto like this, who needs a main course!

SERVES 6 TO 8

- ☐ Seafood Pasta Salad
- ☐ Fagioli alla Toscana—White beans and tuna salad
- ☐ Caponata—Sicilian eggplant salad
- ☐ Bruschetta—Tomato and garlic bread
- ☐ Crostini of Dried Porcini Mushrooms
- ☐ Broiled Red and Green Peppers
- ☐ Fresh Mozzarella with Red and Yellow Tomatoes
- ☐ Platter of Meats: mortadella, soppressata, prosciutto
- ☐ Platter of Cheeses: fresh Parmesan, Gorgonzola, Bel Paese, taleggio
- ☐ Olives

SEAFOOD PASTA SALAD

1 pound fresh medium-sized shrimp, in their shells
1 pound tiny bay scallops
1 pound radiatore, rotelle, rote, farfalle, creste di galli, cappelli del prete, or other small, uniquely shaped macaroni
1 red, green, or yellow bell pepper, cored, seeded, and chopped
1 bunch scallions chopped small
1 large ripe tomato, cored and chopped fine

1 cup minced fresh parsley
1 cup virgin or extra virgin olive oil
1/2 cup freshly squeezed lemon juice (about 4 lemons)
1 tablespoon fresh or 1 teaspoon dried oregano
1 tablespoon fresh or 1 teaspoon dried basil
Salt and freshly ground black pepper to taste

1. Wash and dry the scallops and shrimp. Bring 2 quarts of water to the boil, add the shrimp and scallops, cover, and turn off the heat. Let rest 15 minutes, drain, and peel the shrimp.

2. Cook the macaroni in a large pot of boiling water 10 to 15 minutes, or until it is al dente, or still slightly chewy. Drain, rinse, and let cool.

3. Chop the vegetables and place them in a large salad bowl. Add the shrimp and scallops and the rest of the ingredients. Stir well and marinate for at least 1 hour, stirring often.

FAGIOLI ALLA TOSCANA—WHITE BEANS AND TUNA SALAD

One 16- to 20-ounce can cannellini or other white beans
One 7-ounce can solid white tuna
½ cup finely chopped red onion
⅓ cup minced fresh parsley

⅓ cup extra virgin olive oil
2 tablespoons red wine vinegar
½ teaspoon freshly ground black pepper

1. Buy the best-quality white beans and tuna possible. Cheap tuna and cheap beans will ruin this dish. The tuna must be solid white, not chunk.

2. Place the beans in a mesh strainer and rinse with cold running water. Drain and place in a large salad bowl. Drain the tuna, break it into shreds, and place it in the bowl with the beans. Add the onion and parsley to the bowl and stir.

3. In a separate smaller bowl, mix the oil, vinegar, and pepper. Whisk to form a smooth dressing. Pour over the beans and tuna, stir, and let rest for 30 minutes.

CAPONATA

3 tablespoons olive oil
1 medium-sized yellow or red
    onion, peeled and diced
1 large green or red pepper, cored,
    seeded, and diced
1 medium eggplant, diced
2 stalks chopped fresh celery
1/2 cup minced fresh parsley
2 medium tomatoes, diced

3 tablespoons tomato paste
1/2 cup water
1/2 cup red wine or balsamic
    vinegar, or a combination
2 tablespoons brown sugar
1/3 cup green olives
2 tablespoons capers
1/2 teaspoon each salt and freshly
    ground black pepper

1. Heat the olive oil in a 4-quart saucepan. Add the onion and sauté over medium-high heat for 3 minutes. Add the pepper and eggplant and sauté another 3 minutes.

2. Add the rest of the ingredients and stir well. Cook over medium-high heat for 10 minutes, stirring often. Reduce heat to low and cook for 20 minutes. Turn off heat and let rest 30 minutes. Can be made the day before and refrigerated. Serve at room temperature.

BRUSCHETTA

1 loaf Italian, French, or Swiss
    country bread
4 cloves garlic, each cut in half
    lengthwise

1/2 cup fruity extra virgin olive oil
3 medium-sized very ripe
    tomatoes, finely chopped
Salt and pepper to taste

1. Slice the bread into half-inch-thick slices, ideally 2½ inches by 3 inches. If your loaf is very large, cut the pieces in half.

2. Spread the bread slices on a cookie sheet and toast them in a 500°F. oven for 10 minutes. Don't let them burn.

3. Rub the cut garlic cloves on the toast. Use a basting brush to spread the bread generously with olive oil. Top each slice with a tablespoon of

chopped tomato and sprinkle with salt and pepper. Serve warm or at room temperature.

CROSTINI OF DRIED PORCINI MUSHROOMS

1 cup dried porcini mushrooms
2 cups chopped fresh button
   mushrooms
3 tablespoons olive oil

$1/4$ teaspoon each salt and black
   pepper
1 loaf Italian bread

1. Soak the porcini mushrooms in 1 cup boiling water in a bowl for 20 minutes. Drain and reserve the liquid.

2. Sauté the chopped mushrooms in the olive oil over medium heat for 8 to 10 minutes. Place the drained porcini and sautéed button mushrooms in a food processor and whir for 3 to 5 seconds. Add 2 tablespoons of the reserved soaking liquid and the salt and pepper. Whir again for 5 seconds.

3. Slice the bread into $1/2$- to $3/4$-inch-thick slices, spread the slices on a cooking sheet, and toast them in a 500°F. oven for 10 minutes. Don't let them burn.

4. Spread the mushroom mixture on the slices, place under a heated broiler for 30 seconds, and serve.

BROILED RED AND GREEN PEPPERS

4 large red bell peppers
4 large green bell peppers

$1/4$ cup olive oil

1. Slice the peppers in half lengthwise and remove the seeds and white core material. Place the pepper halves on a broiler pan 6 inches from the heat source.

2. Brush the peppers with olive oil and broil for 5 minutes, turn, and

brush with more olive oil. Broil another 5 minutes. Turn and brush with olive oil. Press the peppers down to flatten them. Broil until the skins are black and charred.

3. Remove the peppers, place them on a plate, and let them cool. Peel off the skins, if desired, and sprinkle with more olive oil. Serve at room temperature.

FRESH MOZZARELLA
WITH RED AND YELLOW TOMATOES

∎━━━━━━━━━━━━━━━━━━━━━━━━━━━━━━━━━━━━━∎

¾ pound fresh mozzarella, fior di latte or regular mozzarella
4 large fresh ripe tomatoes
½ cup minced fresh basil leaves

½ teaspoon freshly ground black pepper
⅓ cup fruity extra virgin olive oil

1. Slice the mozzarella and tomatoes into ⅛-inch-thick slices. Layer the slices in an alternating pattern on a large platter.
2. Sprinkle with fresh basil and black pepper and drizzle with olive oil.

PLATTER OF MEATS

∎━━━━━━━━━━━━━━━━━━━━━━━━━━━━━━━━━━━━━∎

½ pound each mortadella, Genoa salami, soppressata, and prosciutto, or any combination of your favorite Italian cured meats

1. Ask the butcher or deli man to slice the meats as thin as possible.
2. Roll the mortadella and Genoa salami like cigars and place them on a plate of their own.

3. Put the soppressata and prosciutto on separate plates, and layer them in a pinwheel pattern to show off the grain of the fat and lean meat.

PLATTER OF CHEESES

───

$1/2$ pound each Gorgonzola, unaged
    Parmigiano or aged provolone
    or Asiago, Bel Paese, and
    taleggio

1. Gorgonzola is a sharp "blue" cheese. Unaged Parmigiano is still sweet and not so dry and salty as the aged, and aged provolone or Asiago are good substitutes with a similar flavor. Bel Paese is very mild, and taleggio is a ripened cheese like the French Camembert.
2. Place the cheeses on a large platter and let them come to room temperature before you serve them.

OLIVES

───

$1/2$ pound each wrinkled dry-cured
    black olives, purple olives in
    brine, large green olives with
    garlic in brine, and small green
    olives cured in olive oil, garlic,
    and red pepper flakes, or any
    combination of your favorite
    olives

1. Place the olives in separate bowls and set them on the table.

PULLING IT ALL TOGETHER

This is a wonderfully easy menu to serve because you have to cook only two main course dishes. The rest is opening a can or two, combining some easy ingredients, and setting things out on plates. Furthermore, once everything is set out, your work is done and you can enjoy your guests and bask in their praise.

The caponata can be made a day or two ahead of time, or you can make it first and let it sit, covered, on the back of the stove for up to 3 hours. The rest of the menu can be prepared in 1 to 1½ hours, depending on how fast you work.

All of this food except the crostini should be served at room temperature, so I suggest you plan to have everything prepared and everything but the crostini on the table an hour before your guests arrive. This gives you time to freshen up.

First put the dried porcini mushrooms on to soak. Then turn on the oven and toast the bread for the crostini and the bruschetta. Next, broil the peppers. While you are preparing the peppers, remember to chop one for the seafood salad.

Next chop all of the other vegetables for the other dishes: the parsley, scallions, tomato, and garlic for the seafood pasta, the mushrooms for the crostini, the garlic and tomatoes for the bruschetta, and the red onion and parsley for the fagioli salad.

Now, boil and drain the pasta, shrimp, and scallops. Sauté the mushrooms and process them; keep warm. Make the fagioli salad. Finish off the pasta salad. Make the mozzarella and tomato salad. Make the bruschetta and place them on a large platter. Spread the porcini on the bread and place them on a cookie sheet. When your guests have all arrived, place the crostini under the broiler for 30 seconds and serve them.

BEVERAGES. The first things that come to mind are several sweating bottles of icy cold Italian white wine. Soave, Frascati, Verdicchio, Orvieto, Corvo, and Pinot Grigio are all good bets.

Any red wines should be young and lusty. Sicilian Corvo or Etna rosso, Montepulciano di Abruzzo, or Chianti would be good.

AMBIENCE. I imagine this antipasto buffet as an entire meal that is simple, varied, and filling, although you could also use it as the food spread for a cocktail party, letting people nibble as they like. If you are going to serve it as a traditional buffet, lay everything out on a large table on the side of the room. Be sure to have plenty of forks and napkins.

My preferred concept for this meal is to set a large table outdoors in the summertime, under a canopy, tent, or shade tree on a patio. Place all the food and all the wine on the table and let people pass the platters and help themselves. Your guests will soon be telling stories about their travels and great meals they remember in other parts of the world.

■ Cucina Rustica ■

La dolce vita with pasta and seafood.

SERVES 4

- ☐ Orange and Red Onion Salad with Hazelnut Vinaigrette
- ☐ Capellini with Fresh Basil
- ☐ Zuppa di Frutti di Mare—Italian seafood stew
- ☐ Fresh Figs and Ricotta Salata
- ☐ Coffee

ORANGE AND RED ONION SALAD WITH HAZELNUT VINAIGRETTE

2 or 3 large navel oranges
1 medium-sized red onion
4 leaves red leaf lettuce
2 tablespoons olive oil

1 tablespoon hazelnut or walnut oil
1 tablespoon red wine vinegar
Salt and pepper to taste

1. Peel the oranges and remove as much pith and white membrane as possible. Slice the oranges crosswise into ¼-inch-thick slices. You'll need about 3 or 4 slices per serving, 12 to 16 in all.

2. Peel the onion and slice into thin slices. Separate the slices into rings.

3. Wash and dry the lettuce leaves. Place each leaf on a single flat salad plate. Lay the orange slices on top and the onion slices over the orange slices.

4. In a small bowl, mix the olive oil and hazelnut oil, vinegar, and salt and pepper. Whisk to form a creamy dressing. Pour over salads and serve.

CAPELLINI WITH FRESH BASIL

½ pound capellini or angel-hair
  pasta
½ cup olive oil
½ cup finely chopped fresh basil
  leaves

Salt and freshly ground black
  pepper to taste

1. Cook the pasta in a large pot of boiling water until it is al dente or still slightly chewy to the bite.

2. While the pasta is cooking, warm the olive oil in a small saucepan over medium heat for 2 minutes. Add the basil leaves and heat for another minute, stirring often.

3. Drain the pasta and place it in a large bowl. Pour the olive oil and basil over the pasta. Sprinkle with salt and pepper and toss well. Serve in individual warmed flat pasta or soup bowls.

ZUPPA DI FRUTTI DI MARE

2 small live lobsters, 1 to 1¼
  pounds each
1 dozen mussels
1 dozen small littleneck clams
1 small onion, peeled and minced
¼ cup olive oil
2 cloves garlic, peeled and minced
½ cup minced fresh parsley

½ cup dry white wine
2 cups chopped canned Italian
  plum tomatoes
½ teaspoon freshly ground black
  pepper
½ pound small shrimp in their
  shells

1. Bring 1 gallon of water to a boil in an 8-quart pot. Drop the lobsters one at a time in the water and cook each for 1 minute. This kills them instantly. Remove and cool. Chop off the claws and cut the lobsters in half lengthwise, shell and all. Reserve.

2. Scrub the mussels and clams vigorously, and pull the little beards off the mussels. Reserve.

3. Make the sauce for the shellfish in a large 8-quart soup pot: Sauté the onion in olive oil over medium-high heat for 5 minutes. Add the garlic and half the parsley and sauté another 3 minutes. Add the wine, tomatoes, and pepper, reduce the heat to low, and simmer for 10 minutes.

4. Place the clams in a 4-quart pot and add 1 cup of hot water. Turn the heat to high and steam the clams just till they open, 2 to 3 minutes. Remove them carefully, trying to reserve as much clam juice as possible. Steam the mussels open in the same pot and remove them carefully. Discard any clams or mussels that do not open.

5. Place the shrimp and the lobster in the tomato sauce and simmer over medium heat 5 minutes. Add the clams and mussels and their reserved juices. Stir everything together to cover with tomato sauce and cook another 5 minutes over medium-high heat.

6. Use your largest plates and serve each guest a quarter lobster and one claw, plus clams, mussels, and shrimp. Pour the sauce over all. Serve with crusty Italian bread for dipping in the sauce.

FRESH FIGS AND RICOTTA SALATA

8 fresh ripe figs or a jar of figs in
    light syrup
1 pound ricotta salata (firm Italian
    sheep's milk cheese)

Freshly ground black pepper

1. Place 2 figs on each of 4 small dessert plates.
2. Slice the ricotta salata into small wedges. Sprinkle with freshly ground black pepper. Place a wedge of cheese next to the figs and serve.

There are four courses in this meal and quite a bit of work to pull it all together. If you feel it is just too much, omit either the orange and red onion salad or the capellini. If you have the time, do it all, otherwise, take your pick.

Start by getting all the seafood scrubbed and clean. Parboil the lobster and cut it up. Make the tomato sauce for the seafood. You can do all of this early in the day and refrigerate it.

Put the water on to boil for the pasta. If it comes to the boil before you are ready you can always turn it down. Have the basil washed and ready to be chopped and the cheese ready to be grated.

Wash and dry the lettuce for the salad. Make the dressing. Prepare the oranges and red onion, and cover with plastic wrap.

When your guests are arriving, make up the salads. Reheat the tomato sauce. Serve the salads.

After the salad course, return to the kitchen. Put the clams and mussels on to steam. Place the shrimp and lobster in the tomato sauce and turn the heat to very low. Toss the capellini into the boiling water.

Heat the olive oil and basil. Drain the pasta. Toss the oil with the pasta and serve.

After the pasta course, return to the kitchen. Put the clams, mussels, lobster, and shrimp on large plates. Pour the sauce over the seafood and serve. Pass the bread.

Clear the table and serve the figs and ricotta salata.

Serve the coffee.

BEVERAGES. I think you should serve some good mid-range Italian and California wines, both red and white. For the red, try either a California zinfandel or an Italian Cabernet Sauvignon or Chianti. For the white, try the relatively new Galestro wine from Tuscany.

Be sure to have some sparkling water like San Pellegrino on the table.

AMBIENCE. Cucina rustica means rustic cooking, cooking of the small towns, of the home. This menu, because of its emphasis on seafood, is evocative of a seafood platter served in a small seaside town anywhere from Genoa to Naples.

I would give each guest knife and fork, but I would encourage them to use their fingers and hands as utensils for the seafood stew. Make sure they have plenty of bread to scoop up the sauce. Knowing that some tomato sauce may find its way onto the table, I would cover a tablecloth with large sheets of white butcher paper for easy cleanup.

Cucina Rustica

121

Northern Italian

The sophisticated, satisfying cuisine of Northern Italy has taken the country by storm in recent years.

SERVES 4

☐ Risotto with Dried Porcini Mushrooms
☐ Chicken Breasts with Lemon, Capers, and Herbs
☐ Braised Escarole
☐ Bowl of Grapes and Biscotti
☐ Espresso and Anisette

RISOTTO WITH DRIED PORCINI MUSHROOMS

½ cup dried wild porcini mushrooms
1 small red onion, peeled and finely chopped
3 tablespoons butter
1 cup Arborio rice

1 to 1½ cups chicken stock, homemade, canned, or made with a bouillon cube
Salt and freshly ground pepper to taste

1. Soak the dried mushrooms in 1 cup boiling water for 20 minutes. Remove the porcini and strain the liquid through a sieve and reserve.

2. Make the risotto in a 2- to 3-quart saucepan. Sauté the onion in the butter for 3 minutes. Add the Arborio rice and sauté for another 3 minutes over medium heat.

3. Add ½ cup of the chicken stock and stir until all the liquid is absorbed. Turn the heat to low and add another ½ cup stock, stirring until the liquid is absorbed.

4. Chop the mushrooms and stir them into the rice. Add ½ cup of the strained mushroom soaking liquid and stir until it is absorbed. Add the remaining ½ cup mushroom liquid and stir until it is absorbed.

5. Check the rice. It should be tender but al dente, slightly chewy to the bite. If it is ready, sprinkle on the salt and pepper and serve immediately. If not, add another 1/2 cup of the stock and stir until it is absorbed. Total cooking time for the risotto should be 15 to 20 minutes.

CHICKEN BREASTS
WITH LEMON, CAPERS, AND HERBS

■———————————————————————————————————————■

8 medium-sized chicken cutlets or
    4 boneless and skinless
    chicken breast halves
1 cup flour
1/2 cup vegetable oil
2 tablespoons butter
2 tablespoons olive oil
2 tablespoons minced fresh parsley

2 tablespoons tiny nonpareil capers
2 tablespoons minced fresh basil
Juice of 1 lemon
1/2 cup chicken stock, homemade,
    canned, or made with a
    bouillon cube
Salt and pepper to taste

1. To make your own chicken cutlets, place a single breast half flat on the cutting board in front of you. Place one hand flat on top of the breast. Then using a sharp knife with the blade held parallel with the cutting board, slice the breast in half, making two thin cutlets.

2. Place the flour in a large flat bowl and dredge the cutlets in the flour, shaking off any excess. Heat the vegetable oil in a large heavy skillet and fry the cutlets over medium-high heat 2 minutes on each side. Remove from the pan, cover, and keep warm.

3. Dump the frying oil out of the pan and add the butter and olive oil to the same pan. Add the parsley, capers, and basil and cook over medium heat for 1 minute, stirring often.

4. Add the lemon juice, chicken stock, and salt and pepper. Bring the sauce to the boil and cook over high heat for 2 minutes, scraping up any browned bits and making a smooth creamy sauce. Pour over the chicken cutlets and serve.

BRAISED ESCAROLE

1 head escarole or 1 pound
    broccoletti di rape
2 cloves garlic, peeled and minced

¼ cup olive oil
Salt and pepper to taste

1. Separate the escarole head into leaves and wash thoroughly. Pare off any bruised ends or tips and chop into 2-inch-long pieces. Do the same with broccoletti di rape, making sure to use all the stems and leaves.

2. Choose a pot or stainless-steel skillet that has a tight-fitting lid. Sauté the minced garlic in the olive oil over medium-high heat for 1 minute. Add the escarole or broccoletti and sauté for another 2 minutes.

3. Add ¼ cup water, cover the skillet or pot, turn the heat to low, and cook for 10 minutes.

4. Remove the vegetables to a large serving bowl and let them come to room temperature. Add salt and pepper to taste. Vegetables like this are almost always served at room temperature in Italy.

This is a very light and easy dinner to make. The risotto takes the most work because you have to stir it so frequently. The chicken breasts take only 5 minutes to cook and the escarole only 10. You can spend most of your time choosing the biscotti and arranging the bowl of grapes.

First put the mushrooms on to soak. Then arrange the biscotti, grapes, and liqueurs on a side table. Just before your guests arrive, cook the chicken breasts and make the sauce, but don't combine them. Cover the breasts with foil and keep them warm. Braise the escarole.

After you have made the guests comfortable, start making the risotto. At the point where you add the mushrooms to the risotto, get the guests to the table. Risotto has to be served as soon as it is done.

Serve the risotto. Then go back to the kitchen and heat the sauce for the breasts. Serve the breasts and the escarole.

Clear the table and bring on the biscotti and bowl of grapes. If you are lucky enough to live near an Italian bakery, just ask for an assortment of biscotti, which are plain cookies. If not, look for the Stella D'Oro brand of cookies in the supermarket and make your own selection. Try to get three different colors and sizes of grapes. Grapes with seeds have the most flavor, but not everyone likes seeds.

Make the espresso in an espresso pot or use a drip or Melitta-type coffee maker. Do not use a percolator pot because it simply boils the coffee. For the liqueurs, I would set out a bottle of licorice-flavored Sambuca or anisette, a bottle of Frangelico, made with hazelnuts, and a bottle of Amaretto, flavored with almonds.

BEVERAGES. Even though this is a rice and chicken menu, I would serve wines from the northern Piemonte section of Italy. Ask the wine merchant for his best-quality Barolo, Barbaresco, or Nebbiolo d'Alba. These wines are rich and very flavorful. If none of these is available and your wine merchant knows Italian wines, let him pick a Dolcetto, a Barbera d'Asti, or one of the newer Cabernet Sauvignons now being grown in Piemonte.

AMBIENCE. When I think of Northern Italian food I think of the elegance of Venice or Milan. This is an Italian meal with no tomato sauce. This calls for a white linen tablecloth, polished silverware, your best china and crystal, plus white tapered candles.

I would dress the room with a striking but not overly tropical flower arrangement—yellow or white roses, lilacs, multicolored chrysanthemums.

My musical choice would be Italian opera, such as *The Marriage of Figaro*, *The Barber of Seville*, or *L'Italiana in Algeri*.

Sparkling New Year's Eve

Put on your tuxedo or formal dress and be
Nick and Nora, Fred and Ginger.
This is a once-a-year thrill,
and it's worth it.

SERVES 6

- ☐ Smoked Salmon Plate with Toast Points, Capers, and Lemon
- ☐ Blini with Caviar
- ☐ Rack of Lamb with Celeriac Purée
- ☐ Chocolate Mousse

SMOKED SALMON PLATE
WITH TOAST POINTS

¾ to 1 pound presliced smoked
    salmon
6 slices best-quality whole wheat
    or crusty French bread, toasted

3 lemons
1 small jar tiny capers,
    approximately 2 ounces

1. Arrange 2 or 3 very thin slices of smoked salmon on each flat salad plate. Slice a piece of toast in half diagonally and lay a half on either side of the salmon.

2. Cut the lemon into quarters, remove the seeds, and place a wedge on either side of the toast. Place a tiny spoonful of capers in the middle of the plate on top of the salmon. Repeat for all 6 plates and serve.

BLINI WITH CAVIAR

FOR THE PANCAKES:
1¼ cups buttermilk
4 tablespoons (¼ cup) melted
    butter
2 eggs
¾ cup buckwheat flour
¼ cup all-purpose flour
2 teaspoons baking powder

1 teaspoon granulated sugar
¼ teaspoon salt
One 8-ounce container sour cream
    or crème fraîche
2 ounces Beluga, Sevruga, or
    Oestra caviar
½ stick (¼ cup) unsalted butter,
    melted

1. Make the pancakes: Mix the buttermilk, 2 tablespoons melted butter, and eggs in a medium mixing bowl. In a separate bowl, mix the two flours, baking powder, sugar, and salt.

2. Pour the wet ingredients into the dry and stir just enough to incorporate and form a creamy batter. The batter will run a bit, making your blini slightly irregular. Nobody cares. Do the best you can.

3. Fry the blini as pancakes 3 inches in diameter. Use a large skillet to fry 3 at a time. Use just enough of the remaining butter to keep them from sticking. Remove and keep warm. Repeat.

4. To serve, place 2 or 3 buckwheat pancakes on a plate. Drizzle with melted butter. Top each with a tablespoon of sour cream or crème fraîche and top that with ¼ teaspoon caviar.

RACK OF LAMB

3 racks of lamb
1 clove garlic, peeled and split
3 tablespoons olive oil

2 teaspoons dried thyme
1 teaspoon each salt and freshly
    ground black pepper

1. Have the butcher crack the chine bone so that you can carve the racks into chops at serving time. Have the butcher French-cut the ribs so the thin bones are exposed.

2. Preheat the oven to 400°F. Rub the meat with the cut garlic and olive oil. Sprinkle with dried thyme, salt, and pepper.

3. Place the lamb in a low-sided roasting pan and put in the oven. Cook 15 to 20 minutes for medium-rare. Remove from the oven, cover with foil, and let rest 5 to 8 minutes.

4. Carve the rack into chops by slicing down between the ribs and through the cracked chine bone. Serve 2 or 3 on a plate for each person.

CELERIAC PURÉE

2 or 3 medium-sized celeriac or celery roots (if you can't find celeriac, you may substitute rutabaga or turnips)
½ cup half-and-half or milk

2 tablespoons softened butter
2 tablespoons grated Parmesan cheese
Salt and pepper to taste

1. Wash the celeriac and place, unpeeled, in a medium-sized saucepan and cover with water. Bring to a boil, cover, reduce the heat to medium, and simmer for 15 minutes. Drain, peel, and cut into chunks.

2. Place the celeriac chunks in a food processor. Add the half-and-half or milk, butter, and cheese. Process to form a smooth purée. You may need to add more half-and-half or milk. Add the salt and pepper, stir, and return to the saucepan. Reheat the purée slightly just before serving, either on top of the stove or in the oven.

CHOCOLATE MOUSSE

One 6-ounce package semisweet
  chocolate
4 eggs, separated

1 teaspoon vanilla extract, dark
  rum, or Cognac

1. Break up the chocolate into small pieces and place them in the top of a double boiler. Add 2 tablespoons hot water. Place the top of the double boiler over slowly simmering hot water and stir constantly until chocolate is melted. Remove immediately from heat and let cool.

2. In separate bowls, whip the whites until stiff; thoroughly beat the egg yolks. Slowly, bit by bit, add the cooled chocolate to the egg yolks, stirring constantly. Add the vanilla.

3. Carefully fold the egg whites into the chocolate-and-yolk mixture. Spoon the mixture into 6 individual dessert cups, glasses, or bowls. Put in the refrigerator and chill 12 hours or overnight.

PULLING IT ALL TOGETHER

The biggest problem with cooking a meal on New Year's Eve is that you will be all dressed up and either beautiful or handsome. The solution is to do as much as you can in advance and wear a smock or large apron to cover your clothes.

Dress formally. That's right. Put on a tuxedo or evening dress. It's fun. Everyone will like it and you will see sides of your friends' personalities that were previously unknown to you. This menu is for 6 people but it is easily expandable for a maximum of 12 with really no more work for you.

You might as well make the mousse the night before or early in the day because it needs 12 hours to set in the refrigerator.

Set the table early in the day. That way it is finished, all problems have been worked out, and you can enjoy looking at your pretty things all day long.

Before you get dressed you should make the celeriac purée. Cover it and place it in the refrigerator. Make the buckwheat pancakes for the blini. Cover them carefully with foil and let them rest at room temperature.

Make the toast for the smoked salmon plate. Rub the herbs and oil on the lamb, cover with foil, and let rest at room temperature. Now, go get dressed, but don't forget to put the champagne in the refrigerator.

When your guests arrive, hand them a glass of champagne, get them comfortable, and head for the kitchen. Put your smock on.

Preheat the oven for the lamb. Get the celeriac purée out of the refrigerator. While the oven is heating up, place the pancakes, carefully wrapped in foil, in the oven to heat. Make up all the salmon plates. Remove the blini from the oven and put the lamb in the oven. Serve the salmon.

Return to the kitchen and make up the blini plates. Check your time, but the lamb should be just about done. When it is, remove from the oven. Put the celeriac purée in the oven. Serve the blini.

Return to the kitchen and carve the lamb. Put the lamb on plates with the celeriac purée and serve. After that serve the mousse.

BEVERAGES. Champagne, champagne, and more champagne. If you can afford it, get Dom Pérignon, Mumm, or Moët. At least get one bottle of expensive champagne and drink it yourself or serve it to your guests when they first arrive.

Champagne is only champagne when it is made in the Champagne district of France. That leaves room for a lot of óutstanding sparkling wines from other parts of the world. There are some very good Blanc de Blancs sparkling wines, made in France from chardonnay grapes, and at a good price.

Spain also produces some very good sparkling wines. Freixenet, Cordoníu, and Segura Viudas are good names.

California has become a good producer of sparkling wines, especially now, since the Europeans have begun making it there. Look for Chandon, Korbel, Domaine Mumm, Gloria Ferrar, and Schramsberg.

AMBIENCE. This is the night to put out your best tableware and be as formal as you can possibly be. Get out all those crystal bowls and silver platters you received at your wedding or collected along the way. What you don't have, borrow from family or friends.

You should have tall white candles on the table and a nice bouquet of flowers in the room.

Music during the meal should be quiet and instrumental. Classical is a good choice. Vivaldi, Handel, Hayden, Mozart, and piano music by Chopin or Beethoven would be nice. As the evening approaches midnight, be sure to have some Guy Lombardo on hand.